*In Search of*
# Ancient
# Alaska

# In Search of

# Ancient
# Alaska

SOLVING THE MYSTERIES OF THE PAST

## Ellen Bielawski, Ph.D.

ALASKA NORTHWEST BOOKS®
Anchorage ▪ Portland

# to Vernita, Sally, Jane, Paul, Scott, Dave, Jane, and Dick, mentors all

Text © 2007 by Ellen Bielawski

Photo credits are listed with the individual photographs.

The petroglpyh image on the front cover, half- title, and title pages appears with the permission of the USDA Forest Service, Alaska Region.

The chapter opening photographs show dioramas on display at the Anchorage Museum of History and Art. The dioramas were photographed by Chris Arend. The author accepts no responsibility for the accuracy of the material culture or environmental contexts portrayed.

LIBRARY OF CONGRESS CATALOGING-IN-PUBLICATION DATA

Bielawski, E.

In search of ancient Alaska : solving the mysteries of the past / by Ellen Bielawski.
p. cm.
Includes bibliographical references and index.
ISBN-10 0-88240-591-8   ISBN-13 978-0-88240-591-9 (softbound)
1. Indians of North America—Alaska—Antiquities. 2. Indians of North America—Material culture—Alaska. 3. Indians of North America—Alaska—Social life and customs. 4. Alaska—Antiquities. I. Title.

E78.A3B54 2004
979.8'01—dc22                                        2004012007

Alaska Northwest Books®
An imprint of Graphic Arts Center Publishing Company
P.O. Box 10306, Portland, Oregon 97296-0306
503-226-2402
www.gacpc.com

President/Publisher: Charles M. Hopkins
General Manager: Douglas A. Pfeiffer
Associate Publisher: Sara Juday
Editorial Staff: Timothy W. Frew, Tricia Brown, Jean Andrews, Kathy Howard, Jean Bond-Slaughter
Production Coordinator: Susan Dupere
Editor: Linda Gunnarson
Maps: Gray Mouse Graphics
Designer: Andrea Boven Nelson, Boven Design Studio, Inc.

Printed and bound in the United States of America

# Contents

# *Acknowledgments*

Andromeda Romano-Lax and Bill Sherwonit both helped conceive and support this book. Peter Fleischer shared the trials and tribulations of field research. Professor Don Dumond provided great assistance with photos and illustrations. Michael Corrigan proved quick and able in research assistance. Linda Gunnarson edited well and with extreme patience. Jana Harcharak, Vernita Herdman, Gordon Pullar, Janice Ryan, Barbara Svarny-Carlson, and Martha Vlasoff all graciously taught me much more about The People than any artifact could. My warmest thanks to you all.

# A Good Quality of Life

by Moses P. Gabriel

The first historic migration probably took place during a period of time when there was a double link between the lands of western Europe and eastern Asia. The people say that during that remote age, trees and vegetation were scarce in Alaska. The area was blanketed with herbaceous plants, short and knee-high grasses, and scattered clumps of shrubs. Hunters and hunted alike were able to see for great distances. Both man and animal could hear sounds at a great distance, as there were no large trees to block the passage of sound waves.

The first group of migrants must have been extremely curious about their new surroundings. They were greeted by an abundant source of food, consisting of both large game and smaller animals. There were great flocks of waterfowl and many other birds that were easily hunted by the new residents of the land.

Mighty rivers, swift and treacherous, and magical, mirror-like lakes and smaller creeks and sloughs were teeming with a wide variety of fish, including many of our present-day game fish, such as pike and salmon.

Long summer months, filled with seemingly endless sunlight, caused certain areas of the land to yield a great variety of wonderfully delicious berries and numerous edible plants. There were huge quantities of edible roots; there was juicy sap from the young willow shoots, and a variety of mushrooms defying description.

The Nantsaii clans were very pleased with the virgin land and with the ease of their subsistence. A good quality of life seemed reasonably certain, and they settled on that great, magnificent, resource-rich land—ancient Alaska.

—Excerpted from *Gwich'in History*

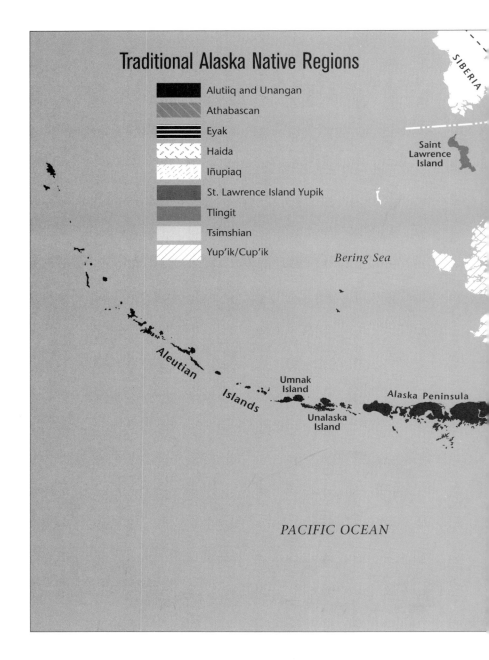

## Traditional Alaska Native Regions

- Alutiiq and Unangan
- Athabascan
- Eyak
- Haida
- Iñupiaq
- St. Lawrence Island Yupik
- Tlingit
- Tsimshian
- Yup'ik/Cup'ik

SIBERIA

Saint Lawrence Island

*Bering Sea*

Aleutian Islands

Umnak Island

Unalaska Island

Alaska Peninsula

*PACIFIC OCEAN*

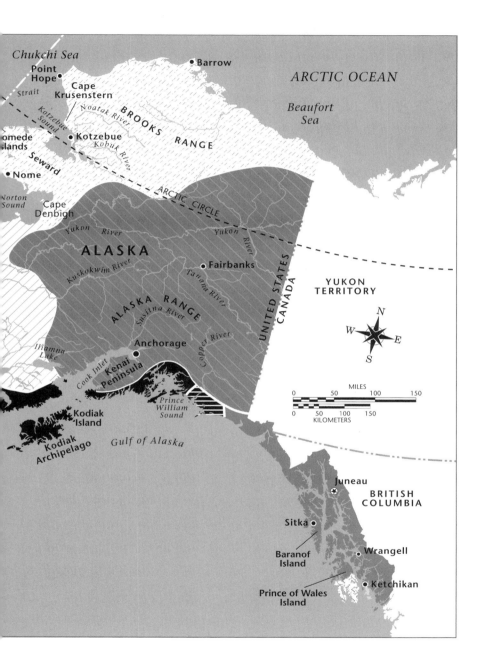

Chukchi Sea

Point Hope •

Cape Krusenstern

Strait

Kotzebue Sound

Noatak River

BROOKS RANGE

omede lands

• Kotzebue

Kobuk River

Seward

• Nome

Norton Sound

Cape Denbigh

ARCTIC CIRCLE

Yukon River

Yukon River

ALASKA

Kuskokwim River

• Fairbanks

Tanana River

ALASKA RANGE

Susitna River

Copper River

Iliamna Lake

• Anchorage

Cook Inlet

Kenai Peninsula

Kodiak Island

Prince William Sound

Kodiak Archipelago

Gulf of Alaska

• Barrow

ARCTIC OCEAN

Beaufort Sea

UNITED STATES

CANADA

YUKON TERRITORY

N
W      E
S

MILES
0        50        100        150

0     50    100    150
KILOMETERS

Juneau ✪

BRITISH COLUMBIA

Sitka •

Baranof Island

• Wrangell

Prince of Wales Island

• Ketchikan

*Introduction*

# The Great Past
# of the Great Land

Alaska's archaeology holds the key to two mysteries of human experience: human adaptation to northern latitudes, and early human migrations from Asia to North and South America.

Whether passing through Alaska to more southerly lands, or settling in for centuries, people have always adapted to extremes: light and dark, water and ice, thick forest and windswept tundra, a glut of fish, game, birds, and berries, or none. Whereas animals adapt primarily physically to their environments, humans adapt primarily through culture. Culture includes the size and structure of families and communities; beliefs and practices, such as spiritual and health rituals; the technology people use to feed and shelter themselves, and to play; intellectual and practical knowledge; and art and music.

Today, the descendants of Alaska's first Native peoples consider themselves members of five distinct groups. In each of their languages, the Native groups' names for themselves in some form mean "The People." From west to east these are:

- Alutiiq, including the Unangan of the Aleutian Islands and the Alutiiq of Kodiak, the Alaska Peninsula, Lower Cook Inlet, and Prince William Sound
- Iñupiaq of northwest Alaska and the Arctic Coast
- Yup'ik/Cup'ik of the Bering Sea Coast
- Athabascan of Interior Alaska and Upper Cook Inlet
- Eyak, Tlingit, Haida, and Tsimshian of Southeast Alaska and the Copper River Delta.

All of The People held their past in oral histories. Their laws, rules, traditions, science, and stories were not written down. Such oral history is one source for learning about The People's past. Another is archaeology, the scientific study of the artifacts, home sites, rock paintings, and everything else that survived The People. Archaeologists study the remains of past cultures. Most of this "archaeological record" consists of the tools for daily living, because most other aspects of human culture are not preserved in the archaeological record. People who study past cultures rely on artifacts and their context to infer the social, spiritual, intellectual, and ritual life of the people who left behind those artifacts. Linguistics tells us about the history and relationships of languages, which tells us something about the history and relationships of people. Rarely, human burials discovered by accident (and carefully reinterred with the appropriate spiritual ceremony) tell us something about how those people lived and died long ago.

All these sources complement and sometimes contradict one another, telling the same story in different ways. Each helps to answer the same questions: Who were the people of the past? When did they arrive in what we now call Alaska? Were they on their way somewhere else—south toward Tierra del Fuego or east toward Greenland? Or did they simply, gradually, drift east and north from Central Asia as the animals they hunted did? Who among the "precontact" peoples—those who lived in Alaska before Europeans arrived and met and wrote about them—are ancestral to Alaska's indigenous peoples?

When we consider Alaska over the past 12,000 years, we are trying to understand an unfinished tapestry by looking at a very few threads gathered from oral history, archaeology, and linguistics. Hundreds of oral histories have been archived, and Native elders continue to record their stories. Archaeologists have excavated key sites throughout the state. We study Alaska's "precontact" past, before European explorers—beginning with Vitus Bering's brief visit in 1741—visited and wrote of Alaska. The "postcontact" period began at a different time for each of the Native groups. Explorers first contacted the Alutiiq between 1750 and 1780; the Eyak/Tlingit/Haida region between 1775 and 1800; the Yup'ik between 1780 and 1840; some Athabascan groups between 1840 and 1860, some even later; and the Iñupiaq between 1850 and 1870. Looking back before contact, we see only a roughly woven tapestry that depicts early peoples' lives. Sources of evidence are still few and scattered relative to the size

## Look, Don't Touch

*What to Do and Who to Contact if You Find Archaeological Remains or Visit Archaeological Sites*

**A**ny disturbance to prehistoric and historic sites on public land

*This Alaska Peninsula site had to be sealed after looters disturbed it, but there is no way to replace what was taken.* (PHOTO BY ELLEN BIELAWSKI)

is illegal. Since nearly 90 percent of Alaska is federal or state public land, it is best to follow the practice of "Look, don't touch." Materials can be removed from private land *only with the permission of the landowner*, but local law often prohibits this. Even if artifacts come from private land, *it is illegal to sell or purchase them*.

of Alaska's landscape and the length of time since people first arrived here. But this is how archaeology and oral history proceed: from one find or Native story to the next, until a pattern takes shape, with many misleading clues along the way.

Growing up in Alaska made me wonder how people came to live here long ago. The land is incomparably beautiful, but the seasons are extreme. What did aboriginal people need to live? What did they need to know, and how did they discover it? My curiosity about the original peoples of the Far North has taken me all over the circumpolar world and earned me a

Five federal laws protect all archaeological remains on federal land:

- Antiquities Act of 1906
- Federal Land Policy and Management Act of 1976
- Archaeological Resources Protection Act of 1979
- Native American Graves Protection and Repatriation Act of 1990
- Theft of Government Property (62 Stat. 764; 18 U.S.C. 1361)

The Alaska Historic Preservation Act protects remains on state land. Penalties for breaking these laws range from a minimum fine up to $250,000 and/or ten years in jail.

You can help protect the archaeological record and learn more about the past by contacting local authorities if you see any apparently unrecorded sites, features, or artifacts during your travels. If you see any evidence of site disturbance and/or artifact looting, call 1-800-478-2724, the Archaeological Resources Crime Hotline.

doctorate in arctic archaeology. Along the way, I have lived, hunted, gathered, prayed, and traveled with Native people. They have taught me much and shared their histories with me, and I have been able to share some of the techniques of archaeology with them.

People always ask me two questions about archaeology: "What's the neatest thing you ever found?" and "How do you know where to look?"

The first question is easy to answer. No single artifact, no matter how aesthetically pleasing nor how efficient its design, compares with the entire adaptation of northern peoples. It is the sum of tiny puzzle pieces from their past that is exciting. The puzzle tells a story of elegant, ingenious inventions suited to a land equal in beauty and risk. While I map tent rings on bare gravel ridges in an arctic wind, or tweeze carbon bits from the remains of ancient cooking fires, I celebrate the entire adaptation Alaska's Native peoples developed over millennia.

The second question also has a simple answer: "common sense." What do people need when they are camping, living, hunting, gathering, or praying somewhere? Are water, shelter, food, and spiritual sustenance available? Are there enough of these to support a community? People are social animals. Could a small group of one or two families live here, or several hundred? For how long, and at what times of year? How did they cache enough food to carry them through lean seasons?

But you can apply common sense to the question only if you can picture what the land was like thousands of years ago. That's where science and training complement common sense and imagination. I have learned to read the land and water I travel for signs of the way it was long ago, and to rely on experts who study and reconstruct land and seascapes from the past. Was that high ridge originally on the edge of an ocean? Might that steep river bluff contain a prehistoric campsite, buried with silt when the river changed course? Questions like these lead archaeologists to places that hold the material clues to ancient Alaska.

In this book, we will travel through the past of each of the five present Native regions: Iñupiaq, Yup'ik/Cup'ik, Athabascan,

Alutiiq, and Eyak/Tlingit/Haida/Tsimshian. From the descriptions of artifacts and sites, try to imagine what the land, water, and ice were like thousands of years ago. What animals, fish, and other species lived there? How did people adapt to their present or changing environments?

Much as archaeology strives to be scientific, it is not possible to think about life among people thousands of years ago without using one's imagination. But archaeologists don't indulge in science fiction. Rather, we extend what we know from living cultures—that is, the technological, social, spiritual, economic, and intellectual ways of doing things that make up each culture's unique identity, as well as their adaptations to their environment—to help interpret the material culture left by peoples of the past. *Material culture* is the term archaeologists use for the artifacts of past peoples—things that people made. Archaeological sites and features typically contain artifacts; they may also contain faunal material—bone scraps from animals that people ate—and human remains—the bones or tissue of people who died at the site or were laid to rest there after death. To interpret the past lifeways of people, archaeologists rely on material culture evidence, analysis of faunal remains, and analysis of human remains when this is appropriate. All of these make up an *archaeological culture.* "Material culture" refers *only* to the manufactured items or fragments of them.

The older a site, the fewer remains we find. Generally, the oldest archaeological sites consist only of objects made of stone, although we know the people who made those artifacts must

# Bringing the People and Sacred Objects Home

## Alaska Natives and the Native American Graves Protection and Repatriation Act

Early in the twentieth century, the federal government moved to protect the sites, graves, and artifacts left by Native Americans from looting for the sale of artifacts and bones, and from unscientific excavation and personal collecting. While the Antiquities Act of 1906 provided minimal protection for precontact remains, unfortunately it relied on treating First Americans' remains as public property, cared for by the federal government. From 1906 to 1990, the Antiquities Act allowed many federally funded institutions—such as the National Park Service, museums, and universities—to collect human remains and sacred objects and keep them.

Native tribes worked for nearly a century to gain back control of their ancestors' graves, human remains, and sacred objects. The Native American Graves Protection and Repatriation Act of 1990 (NAGPRA) mandates the return of human skeletal material and sacred objects from federally funded institutions to the tribes who document their relationship with their ancestors through oral and in some cases written history. Through NAGPRA, many of the human remains that collectors took from Alaska have been returned and reburied. The act also provides for the protection of Native American graves found in the future on federal and tribal lands.

In cases of relatively recent disturbance to Native graves, documenting the connection between today's tribes and the remains of their ancestors is straightforward. Often the excavator's field notes describe in detail the location and character of the burial ground source of skeletal remains. In this case, the connection, or "cultural affiliation," between the remains and today's tribe is clear.

Questions arise when prehistoric human remains without a clear connection to a modern tribe are found on federal or tribal land. The case of Kennewick Man is the hotly debated, well-publicized case of a single skeleton. Five Washington State tribes argued that the 9,500-year-old skeleton is their ancestor and that they should properly rebury it. Scientists argued for the right to study the rare find. While the case was being decided, scientists were able to carry out several technical studies. Ultimately, in 2004, federal archaeologists determined that there is enough evidence to consider the skeleton Native American for purposes of NAGPRA, and the remains of Kennewick Man were returned to a group of tribes in the Pacific Northwest, including the Colville, Nez Perce, Umatilla, Wanapum, and Yakima.

have used plants, wood, animal bone, hide, and perhaps shell to make their shelters, clothing, and containers. Such organic material decays quickly, however, and thus is lost to the archaeological record. When pieces of animal bone are found, archaeologists cannot always tell the difference between fragmented faunal remains that people worked into tools and those simply cut, burned, or shattered in the process of food preparation. Deterioration of both artifacts and faunal remains over time complicates interpretation.

Archaeologists study living cultures and historic cultures

*Archaeologists found this 2,000-year-old stone lamp*
*in three fragments on the Alaska Peninsula.*
(PHOTO BY DON DUMOND)

(those documented in oral history, photographs, and written records) for clues about material cultures of the past. For example, consider the oil lamp that the Iñupiaq and Yup'ik relied on for heat and light.

When an archaeologist finds a fragment of stone that looks like part of an oil lamp, what does she or he surmise? What did people need to know—in other words, what knowledge was part of their intellectual and technological culture so that they could make, fuel, and use such a lamp? They needed to know

*Tufts of cotton grass, twisted together, were used as oil lamp wicks.*
(PHOTO BY BILL SHERWONIT)

where to find the right kind of rock for pecking, grinding, or polishing into a lamp shape, perhaps with a wick rest. They may have known the original source of the stone, or they may have traded with neighboring peoples for it. They needed hard, usually granitic rock to work the softer stone into a shape that would hold lamp oil. If they quarried soapstone, for example, they probably knew that it is soft and easy to sculpt when first quarried and that it hardens after exposure to air. For oil, they needed the blubber of marine mammals, which meant they had the knowledge and technology for hunting such animals. And they needed material for the lamp wick. Historically, Iñupiaq and Yup'ik used cotton grass and other organic, burnable materials for wicks. So people had to know what plants or other organic material could absorb the oil, then burn with it, in order for the lamp to function.

Thus, the archaeologist who finds only a fragment of a stone lamp infers that the people who made and used it also knew and used many other things to make the lamp functional. By connecting the material culture of the archaeological record with the knowledge we have from historic and living cultures of how it must have been used, we imagine a picture of past lifeways, even though the material culture we find in sites, features, and artifacts consists only of lithic remains, or pottery, or bone, minus the sinew for lashing and sewing, the hides that were sewn, the wicks for lamps, and the hide covers for circles of stone that are all that remain from tent sites.

When reading about Alaska's earliest cultures, you will see lists of objects that early peoples made and left behind. Such lists are static. To understand the lives of the people who made and used prehistoric artifacts, you need to imagine people going through the daily routine of life. You must imagine all of the parts of their homes, furnishings, tools and utensils that their lives required. Organic items like clothing and footwear made of animal hide, the wooden shafts of arrows, spruce root or grass baskets, wooden bowls or bark containers, have not survived the passage of time. We must imagine how these soft items held together the hard artifacts that remain as the archaeological record. To help you visualize the living rather than static material culture, the watercraft of Alaska's Native people as we know it from oral history is presented in detail. Watercraft demonstrate well the detailed knowledge of plants, trees, and animals that the ancestors of today's Native groups must have had to adapt in ancient Alaska. Other examples exist in traditional hide clothing, in hunting, butchering, and cooking implements, in settlement patterns and other aspects of cultures that have evolved over time.

Then, whenever and wherever you travel in Alaska, from the petroglyphs near Ketchikan to the whale-bone pit houses on the Arctic Coast, you can imagine the lives of people who were there long before you.

This book concludes with some recommendations for digging deeper in search of ancient Alaskans. References and resources abound for places where you can retrace ancient trails and visit precontact sites, cultural centers, interpretive sites, and museums in Alaska. There you can see and hear in person what Native elders know, and what archaeologists, linguists, and others have learned about the mysteries of the past.

# Chapter 1

# Tundra Plains and Mammoth Game: Beringia and the Earliest Alaskans

**H**ow long ago did people first live in what we now call Alaska? What brought them here? What environment did they adapt to?

Alaska's Native groups each have oral histories that speak of how they came to be in this land. Native histories tell of the Earth's creation, sometimes from water, sometimes from nothing; of the ancestry of the moon and stars; of the creation of animals and humans; of clans and the animals and places with which they are associated.

These oral histories differ among groups, but they have in common the absence of measured, or calendrical, time that archaeologists and historians of the written word rely on to interpret the archaeological record. On our Gregorian calendar, we recognize that people lived in Alaska as early as 12,000 years ago. From that time through about 4,000 years ago, the archaeological record in Alaska is sparse.

Determining the age of archaeological collections is a technical task that relies on several methods. Archaeological dates are reported in terms that vary widely among archaeologists. In this book, I state the age of archaeological remains in number of years "before the present," or "B.P." This is the designation archaeologists commonly use to express how many years ago an artifact, a site, or a feature such as a hearth or house was in use and, by inference, how long ago the people who made and used it were alive.

# Archaeological Nomenclature, or, Who Were Those Guys Anyway?

The farther back we travel through time, the less able we are to trace a direct line between the Native people of today and those who lived in Alaska before they appear in written history. Some connections are clear, however. Alaska's Iñupiaq, for example, can trace their ancestry directly to the group of precontact people who settled the Arctic Coast about 1,000 years ago. Iñupiaq oral history and similarities in diet, tools, clothing, and houses between the ancestral group and the Iñupiaq show the relationship over time. On the other hand, there are cultural borderlands throughout Alaska that different groups used at different times—for example, Iñupiaq and Athabascan hunters in the Brooks Range; Tanaina and Alutiiq peoples along Cook Inlet; Eyak and Tlingit in Southeast Alaska. These shared territories mean that material remains found in these places cannot be easily connected to one contemporary group.

Were the people whose earliest remains we find the direct ancestors to Alaska's present-day Native peoples? Ancient tools don't come with ethnic or tribal labels attached. Throughout this book and in any further reading you do on prehistory and archaeology, you will encounter a collection of labels for sets of prehistoric remains. From smallest to most encompassing, some of these are *artifact*, *feature*, *site*, *culture*, and *tradition*. This short list omits many finer distinctions that archaeologists use. An *artifact* is a single object that people have altered from a natural state to one that shows human use. A *feature* is the remains of human use of the landscape—such as a pit house—and the artifacts it includes. A *site* is a cluster of artifacts and/or features.

**Archaeological Nomenclature, or, Who Were Those Guys Anyway?** (cont'd)
Archaeologists define prehistoric cultures and traditions (and their variants) more subjectively than they do artifacts, features, and sites. A *culture* is a grouping of sites, features, and artifacts according to their similarity. A *tradition* may encompass several cultures that may vary widely but share essential elements.

We are not always able to identify archaeological finds through their relationship to a living group of people. Therefore, archaeologists assign special names—names that differ from the names Native people use to describe themselves—to collections of precontact remains. Only when enough evidence points to a direct relationship between a precontact archaeological find and a Native group will archaeologists say that a collection of prehistoric remains is "directly ancestral" to a living group of people.

Throughout this book, you will learn the common names archaeologists have assigned to different precontact groups of people who occupied Alaska before anyone wrote down the aboriginal peoples' names for themselves. Some of the most common names—such as Thule Culture, Arctic Small Tool tradition, and Kachemak Bay tradition—refer to archaeological remains that are widely spread across Alaska and that archaeologists agree have a clear identity in the precontact record.

Archaeologists usually name the remains they find after an outstanding attribute, such as the small stone tools that characterize the tool kits of people who lived along the Arctic Coast from about 4,000 to 1,000 years ago (Arctic Small Tool tradition), or the place they are first found, such as Kachemak Bay (Kachemak Bay tradition).

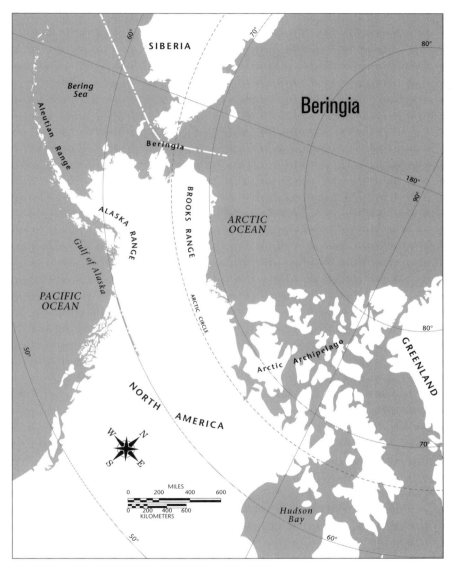

*This map shows the Beringian landmass*

*when sea level was lowest during the most recent great glaciation.*

*Alaska's earliest known archaeological sites are found here.*

It is not possible to connect the material remains of Alaska's earliest people with any specific Native Alaskan oral history; it is also impossible to rule out all connections among them.

Along with wanting to know when and how first peoples lived in Alaska, we want to know why people came to Alaska. Ten-thousand-year-old data tempt us to gross simplicity in our interpretation. There is little we can say with any conviction, and what we "know" now may change with the discovery of more data.

Nowhere are we more challenged to imagine a past world than in seeking to understand Alaska as it was 12,000 years ago, and what it was like for the first several generations of early peoples. To start with, the land was not Alaska as we know it. Periodically between 100,000 years ago to sometime after 14,000 years ago, the Asian and North American continents were connected across what is now the Bering Strait. We call the large landmass of interior Alaska, interior Siberia, and the land connecting them "Beringia."

At times during this long period, the landmass of Beringia stretched from Lake Baikal in Siberia to eastern Alaska. During other, warmer times, the landmass was likely reduced to a narrower "bridge" between the continents. The great ice sheets that covered much of North America and Asia bound Beringia. This glaciation contained so much of Earth's water that sea level was much lower than it is now, which is why the Beringian landmass existed.

Sometime before 12,000 B.P. people first occupied western Beringia (now Siberia) and eventually what is now Alaska.

*13,700-year-old Mesa site projectile point.*
(PHOTO BY MIKE KUNZ)

After the most recent melting of the major ice sheets, the sea rose and flooded Beringia, forming the Bering Sea, the Bering Strait between the Diomede Islands, and the Chukchi Sea. If the first peoples lived along the coasts of Beringia, any trace of them has long been flooded, so we may never know how and when they came. People with an archaeological culture resembling the earliest finds in Alaska lived in western Beringia at least 18,000 years ago. Their adaptation emphasized hunting land mammals.

Beringia was treeless, windy, and likely cold, but it was at times home to very large animals, such as the woolly mammoth, along with bison, horse, musk oxen, camel, antelope, and caribou. Populations of animals and humans were probably sparse. If the people gradually expanded east from Asia, they could have done so without changing their adaptation substantially as they populated central and eastern Beringia.

## A Stone Tool Primer

The vast majority of early archaeological finds are stone tools, whole or in fragments. But not just any rock can be shaped into a good tool. The right kinds of stone vary in color and somewhat in texture, but all share one property: *isotropism*. Simply put, this means that when force is applied, the stone will fracture evenly in all directions. Obsidian (also called black glass), basalt, and various stones called flint, chert, and chalcedony all share this property.

In early Alaskan artifact collections, the most common tool types are:

- Flake—a fragment intentionally removed from a larger stone
- Core—a stone nodule preshaped with flaking so that sharp, narrow blades can be struck from it
- Blade—a narrow, parallel-sided flake struck from a prepared core; can be used as a tool without further working, or may be further shaped for specific purposes
- Microblade, microcore—miniature versions of blades and cores, definitive particularly of the Arctic Small Tool tradition
- Projectile point—a stone shaped to tip an arrow, harpoon, or spear

We have no evidence anywhere that Beringian peoples used watercraft for either traveling or hunting. Even if they did hunt marine mammals, they must also have relied on terrestrial species.

Very few archaeological sites represent the earliest people to live in Alaska. The Mesa site lies in the Brooks Range, in what was eastern Beringia when Mesa was occupied, between 10,300

- Scraper—a tool with sharpened edges, used for scraping hides
- Burin—a mitten-shaped tool used for grooving and incising bone and antler
- Burin spall—a tiny thin flake struck from a burin's engraving point to sharpen the burin

Stone tools are made through percussion flaking—striking the isotropic stone with another rock, the hammer stone—and pressure flaking. For pressure flaking, the core is prepared with a hammer stone. Then another tool, usually a bone or antler punch, is placed on the core platform—its upper, flat surface. The toolmaker strikes the punch with a heavy rock used as a hammer, and the pressure breaks blades or flakes off the core. Archaeologists divide flaked stone tools into two classes—unifacial, meaning that the tool was flaked on only one side, and bifacial, those with flaking on both sides.

From about 4,000 years ago, many Native Alaskans pecked cobbles into oil lamps or even bowls. Softer stone, such as soapstone, was ground and polished into adzes and lamps.

and 11,500 years ago. The earliest strata at the Dry Creek, Broken Mammoth, and Walker Road sites, all just north of the Alaska Range, are comparable in age, dated to between 12,000 and 10,000 B.P. These sites hold the remains of stone hunting tools that are similar to those of early Americans much farther south. The stone tools from the Mesa site include a collection of leaf-shaped (lanceolate) projectile points that are similar to the projectiles of early peoples much farther to the south. Two other sites in Beringia may indicate early peoples. One is in Yukon, at Bluefish Caves, and is dated to 13,000 B.P. Trail Creek Caves, on the Seward Peninsula in northwest Alaska, is dated to 13,000 B.P., but archaeologists disagree on whether human or natural processes created the broken bones there. Some attribute the animal bone fractures to natural processes of freezing and thawing, while others believe that early people intentionally broke the bones in the process of butchering and food preparation.

Such sparse data can tell us little more than that people had arrived in Alaska. Data on the climate, animals, and plants of Beringia tell us that these people had developed an adaptation to nomadic hunting that likely included harvesting plant resources for food and perhaps medicine. We can say very little else about how these early Alaskans lived.

None of these earliest sites includes the core and blade technology that is the hallmark of later Alaskans. About 10,000 years ago, core and blade technology became widely spread throughout Alaska. The technology is essential for people who relied on mobility, stone projectile points for hunting, and

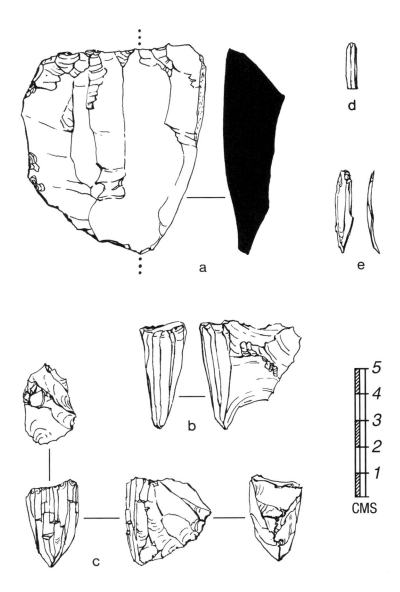

*Examples of Paleoarctic tradition stone tools. Cores a and b are from the earliest strata at the Onion Portage site.*

(ILLUSTRATION BY CAROL STEICHEN DUMOND)

blades for butchering and for cleaning hides for clothing. So sophisticated are the refinements in the manufacture of cores and the many tools struck from them that archaeologists often use the styles of cores and blades to define a prehistoric group, especially because whatever the people had that was made of bone, wood, or hide did not survive the passage of millennia.

Remains dating from the time period 10,000 B.P. to 8000 B.P. fall together in the Paleoarctic tradition. By Paleoarctic times, the Alaska environment was likely one of northern boreal forest, or taiga, and tundra. From Lake Baikal in Siberia to eastern Alaska, this environment supported people who clearly shared similar technologies. The people were land-based hunters, living in small, mobile groups. The sites they left behind seem to represent small camps or hunting look-outs. Their core and blade technology is most likely derived from earlier artifact assemblages in Siberia and northeast Asia, which in turn show connections to northern Japan, north-eastern China, and Mongolia. The Alaskans of the Paleoarctic tradition did not simply pass through Alaska as earlier peoples may have, but settled into a durable adaptation that rested on their ability to move as their food resources did, to harvest enough animals year-round, to cache and freeze food and per-haps to dry it, in order to ensure their survival.

The earliest evidence of the Paleoarctic tradition is in the Akmak assemblage at the Onion Portage site on the Kobuk River, which is dated to about 10,000 B.P. The Paleoarctic tradi-tion is also represented at the Dry Creek site in central Alaska and, on the Bering Sea side of the Alaska Peninsula, at the

Ugashik River drainage, where remains date to 9000 B.P. Five hundred miles separate Onion Portage from the Ugashik sites, but their cultural similarity is clear. Assemblages from both include artifacts consistently part of the Paleoarctic tradition: wedge-shaped microcores, microblades, burins, leaf-shaped bifaces, and core bifaces. Other sites of this tradition vary more in their artifact assemblages but are still clearly part of the Paleoarctic tradition: Healy Lake, Putu on the Arctic Slope, and Batzu Tena on the Koyukuk River. Anangula, in the Aleutians, and the Gallagher Flint Station, on the Sagavanirktok River on the Arctic Slope, have Paleoarctic tradition assemblages except that they lack bifaces. As mentioned earlier, the Paleoarctic tradition shares cultural characteristics with earlier assemblages in Asia. Throughout its duration, the area of Alaska's coast that became, much later, Yup'ik, Cup'ik, and Iñupiaq territory was an extension of Asia stretching east to what is now Alaska; all of that area can be considered Beringia.

Onion Portage is that rare archaeological site where layers of human occupation lie one above the other, in a vertical map of human occupations through time. Such mapping is called "stratigraphy"—literally, writing in the layers. There, archaeologists first discovered the distinctive collection of artifact and feature attributes that is most commonly called the Paleoarctic tradition, the core and blade complex of stone tools that includes the bone-working tools called burins. Other Paleoarctic tradition sites are found throughout Alaska, including on the Chilkat Peninsula in Southeast Alaska and on Baranof and Hecata Islands. As we shall see in the next chapter,

# First Peoples Enter North and South America

What, if any, connection did the first Alaskans have with early settlers elsewhere on the American continents? The Mesa site and some layers of the Broken Mammoth and Dry Creek remains show a similarity to the earliest artifacts found in continental North America. Glaciological evidence indicates that an ice-free corridor may have existed between the major east and west ice sheets of North America. People—as well as land animals and birds—could have made their way along this corridor from Beringia east and south to what are now southern Canada and the United States, and even beyond to South America. Earth scientists are still debating whether or not an ice-free corridor existed, and if it did, if it supported enough animals and plants for people to live on during migrations south.

Several sites elsewhere in North and South America have been dated to earlier than any Alaskan sites. These finds lead many archaeologists to believe that the continents were not settled by overland migrants through Alaska, but through one or a combination of three other possible routes. It is possible that people came from Asia to North America via boats along Beringia's shore and down the Pacific Coast. Archaeologists continue to search for evidence of this route.

People could also have crossed the Pacific from Asia to points in North and South America on long sea voyages. Support for such waterborne migrations comes from archaeologists who have found very early remains on the South American coast as far south as Tierra del Fuego. The age of these sites is hotly debated—the usual state of affairs surrounding the earliest settlement of America. Other archaeologists believe that people who crossed the northern Atlantic Ocean, not the Pacific, first settled North America. This idea is based on well-documented archaeological sites in eastern North America. If either or both of the latter two routes should prove correct, it may mean that the earliest Americans did not arrive via Alaska at all.

These are exciting times in the search for the first peoples to reach North America from the Old World. Glaciers that have advanced several times since the earliest migrations are again receding. As they do, more evidence to answer the question of who first came to the New World, and how, may emerge from under the ice.

Archaeologists group the earliest North and South American remains—from famous sites such as Clovis and Folsom in New Mexico and Agate Basin in Wyoming—in a Paleoindian tradition. Artifacts from these sites share a distinctive characteristic. Their long, thin projectile points bear a "flute"—the linear scar of a final flaking blow struck at the base of the point. Such fluted points have been found in Alaska, but not in Siberia. Many archaeologists include the Mesa and earliest Dry Creek remains in the broader North American Paleoindian tradition. Most of the evidence, and most archaeologists, still support the idea that people entered what is now Alaska via the area we call Beringia.

some of the earliest occupations in the Alutiiq region also share in the Paleoarctic tradition.

Moving forward through time, the next group of people archaeologists can identify bear a collection of archaeological remains called the Northern Archaic tradition. These remains seem to represent an adaptation primarily to an Interior, rather than a marine, environment. This tradition appears in the archaeological record around 6000 B.P. Many archaeologists believe that this tradition contributed little to the later cultures of Alaska, but some believe it may represent distant ancestors to the Athabascan people. Northern Archaic sites are found in the Brooks Range and elsewhere in Interior Alaska.

Only enough archaeological evidence exists of both of the Paleoarctic and Northern Archaic traditions to connect a few far-flung sites to one another on the basis of similarity in their artifact assemblages. From the similarity within each tradition, we infer that the people of each tradition shared aspects of adaptation to the environment of the time. We believe that people of the Paleoarctic tradition were adept at hunting the large and small game on the remnant of the Beringian plain after melting glaciers reduced its size by flooding it. When climatic evidence shows that the boreal forest had expanded to the north, Northern Archaic tradition remains appear in the archaeological record. The people who left behind the artifacts of the Northern Archaic tradition may have moved north better adapted to forest hunting than to tundra hunting; or, the Paleoarctic peoples may have adopted the forest hunting technology from neighbors to the south as their environment became more forested. There's just too little data from this long ago to say.

Moving forward in time throughout Alaska, from about 4000 B.P. onward, the archaeological record begins to show the path toward regional adaptations to specific environments. Someday we may learn more than we know now of any connections between the peoples of the Paleoarctic and Northern Archaic traditions and the later regional groups in Alaska.

# Chapter 2

# From the Aleutians to Prince William Sound: The Alutiiq and Unangan Region

The Alutiiq and Unangan region extends from the far western tip of the Aleutian Islands northeast across the lower Alaska Peninsula and eastward to Prince William Sound. It includes the Kodiak Archipelago. This vast, diverse coastline supported the evolution of two groups of people who shared a remarkable adaptation to a cold ocean but whose languages and material cultures differed substantially. Today their descendants use the general names Alutiiq and Unangan to describe themselves, although they also recall more specific tribal names, such as Ounalashka and Kenaitye. Russian explorers called the Unangan people on the Aleutian Islands and outer reaches of the Alaska Peninsula "Aleuts." Later explorers called the people who lived on Kodiak Island and along Lower Cook Inlet and Prince William Sound "Pacific Eskimos."

Adaptation in the Alutiiq and Unangan region requires the ability to make a living from a cold and wild sea on an ice-free shore year-round. Powerful ocean currents meet in the Gulf of Alaska and along the Aleutian Islands, mixing relatively warm with frigid waters. The result is an almost unbelievably rich marine environment holding a variety of food sources more abundant and varied than those in the Interior or on the Arctic Coast and tundra. Where sea ice forms, in the northern parts of this region, it flows loose and treacherous with the tides. Mountains are steep and hug the shores of deep fjords.

# Alutiiq

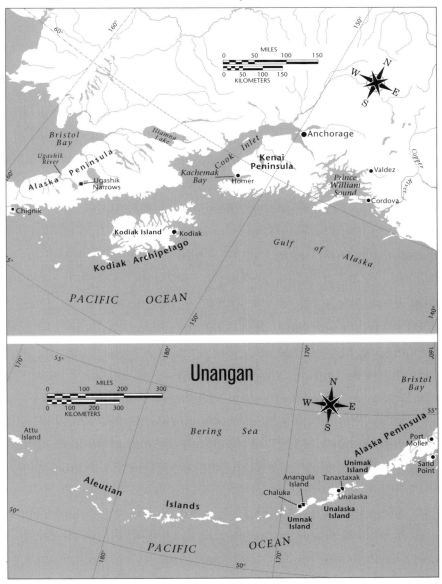

# Unangan

Volcanoes are active on the Aleutian Islands, the Alaska Peninsula, and on the sea floor. Earthquakes are common here, and hot springs not uncommon.

By 9000 B.P. people were living near what is now the city of Unalaska. By 8000 B.P., people were living at the Anangula site, just off the present shoreline of Umnak Island in the eastern Aleutians. These are two of the earliest known coastal sites in North America. The earliest occupation of the deep, stratified Anangula site includes evidence of homes, either permanent or semipermanent. These remains are large, oval-shaped, and about fifteen feet long. They appear to have been excavated into the earth so that the living area was mostly underground. People likely entered and exited these homes through the roof. Archaeologists found sea mammal bones in debris at the site; the only tools preserved were made of stone. The coastal location, the dwelling remains, and the sea mammal bone all suggest that these earliest inhabitants, while sharing much of the stone tool technology of the Paleoarctic peoples farther north, had changed their adaptation significantly as they migrated across Beringia and out into what became the Aleutian Islands. Their ability to harvest the rich resources of the sea here allowed them to stay in one place much more consistently than could the nomadic hunters farther north. Most likely these people had some sort of watercraft because Anangula was already separated from Umnak Island by water by the time the site was first occupied.

By about 6,500 years ago, people were living from the sea on Kodiak Island. Archaeologists assign their sites and artifacts

# Watercraft: Indigenous Adaptation and Legacy

After Beringian and Northern Archaic times, when the regional differentiation began that led eventually to the historic Native Alaskans that European explorers met, we can be fairly sure that people developed watercraft—if they hadn't already. Alaska's coasts, enormous river drainages, and huge lakes dictate the use of watercraft to survive and thrive. Without this, there is no living in the country. One travels on water, or over it when frozen, or over ice to where the water is open. Rivers and lakes are the roads of Alaska's Interior; the ocean is the freeway of the coasts.

We can't know when the first watercraft was invented, nor how it evolved, simply because the raw materials for Alaska Native watercraft are rarely preserved in the archaeological record. Nevertheless, watercraft are wonderful artifacts through which to appreciate similarities and differences among Alaska's Native cultures, and to understand the rich and complex knowledge that early peoples developed in order to make and use their watercraft and to exploit challenging marine and riverine environments.

In the Unangan and Alutiiq region, where the ocean does not freeze, boats that have come to be known as baidarkas were essential to survival year-round. *Baidarka* is a Russian-Aleut word, and "kayak" is the modern term generally used for these craft. The original word for a kayak was something like *iqyax* for a one-hatch kayak and *uluxtax* for a kayak with two hatches.

Both Unangan and Alutiiq baidarkas are made of wood frames covered with sea lion or seal hides. The precontact boatbuilders

## Watercraft: Indigenous Adaptation and Legacy (cont'd)

had to find the right wood—from driftwood in the Aleutians or from alder growing on the Alaska Peninsula. The wooden frames of the long, light craft were made of many small pieces held together with sinew lashing and perhaps with some sort of glue. All the wood had to be cut and planed to the correct size and shape. The earliest boatbuilders must have used stone tools—flaked stone knives and adzes—to prepare the wooden pieces for their boats. Steam was used, historically, to bend and shape wood. It was probably part of precontact boatbuilding as well.

Hide preparation and sewing involved several steps. First the hair had to be removed from the hide. This was done by scraping

*Master boatbuilder Mike Livingston paddles an Alutiiq kayak. He wears an Alutiiq hat with a long brim that shields his face from rain and his eyes from glare. His waterproof rain jacket is made of split intestines that have been dried and sewn together.* (PHOTO BY CLARK JAMES MISHLER)

and/or thoroughly soaking the hide in a mixture of wood ashes and water. Next the people stretched the hides to shape and dry them. Finally, the hides were stretched snugly over the boat's wooden frame and sewn with a waterproof stitch. Additionally, seams may have been caulked with moss and a natural glue or pitch. Historically, Unangan kayaks were painted with red ochre. Their handling and maintenance was an art in itself.

Within each regional style, many local variations probably existed. Two that have survived through the historic decimation of the Alutiiq and Unangan peoples are different bow types. The Unangan bow curves up to a point just in front of the horizontal upper surface of the craft. In contrast, the Alutiiq bow is vertically forked. The lower upturned bow serves as a cutwater, while the upper bow acts as a flotation piece that helps the paddler maneuver the kayak in rough water.

Another part of Alaska Natives' sophisticated adaptation to water that is not preserved in the archaeological record is the training that prepared people to pilot their kayaks. It probably began when children were very young; such training was historically given to Alutiiq and Unangan youth. A prime example of the importance of early training is teaching children to sit in the correct paddler's position. In a kayak, this requires sitting with legs extended, close together and flat inside the kayak's hull. The back must be straight, the kayaker balanced with arms extended holding the double-bladed paddle. The position requires flexibility in the hamstrings and hips and a strong back and abdomen. Traditional Unangan and Alutiiq trained their children to sit in this position while playing games, thus shaping and strengthening the

**Watercraft: Indigenous Adaptation and Legacy (cont'd)**

muscles and the growing bones for skillful use of the kayak.

Master boatbuilder Mike Livingston, who is half Aleut (Unangan), probably says it best, as Jan Steinbright reports in *Qayaqs and Canoes: Native Ways of Knowing*: "Baidarka building is a concept. You take a bunch of tiny little parts of wood as small as you can possibly get them, you lash them together and then you cover it with the hide. The hide is a structural member of the kayak . . . So it's all an engineering feat and an engineering mystery in terms of how they were able to paddle as quickly as they were on such long distances . . . Aleut kayaks were not really cargo ships. They were more like racing hulls. They weren't designed to carry a bunch of weight; they were designed to get from point A to point B, point A usually being the beach and point B being the sea otter or seal. Their purpose was for getting there quickly, making the kill, and returning to shore. They were hunting machines, hunting tools."

to the Ocean Bay tradition. From the common substrate of the Ocean Bay tradition emerged the precontact Unangan tradition and the Kodiak tradition. Along with chipped stone tools, people began to grind and polish slate during this time. This tradition continues for several thousand years and through several variations on both the Kodiak Archipelago and the Alaska Peninsula. Similar human occupations occurred in the region of Kachemak Bay. By about 5,000 years ago, the archaeological record suggests two separate paths of cultural evolution. One leads eventually to the Unangan people, whom

Russian explorers described after 1741, and the other to the Alutiiq culture of the Kodiak Archipelago, the Pacific side of the Alaska Peninsula, and east into Prince William Sound.

Regardless of what we call their material-culture remains, what we want to know is, what were people doing? Unangan ancestors settled at the Chaluka site northeast of Unalaska in the Fox Islands about 4000 B.P. and lived there, as far as archaeologists can tell, continuously from then until historic contact with Europeans. The Chaluka site, like many others in the Aleutians, is a large, deep midden, or refuse heap, containing animal bones discarded from butchered, cooked, and eaten food and all the other detritus of daily life. Although precontact peoples produced far less to throw away than people in industrialized society do, a midden usually contains thousands of unfinished or broken pieces of the material culture. We can imagine that the skin clothing people must have worn would have been discarded once or twice a year, its organic decomposition adding to the midden's mix.

The precontact Unangan people preferred places like the spit where the Chaluka midden lies, along with sheltered bays and the mouths of freshwater streams. When the early Unangan found a location with shelter from ocean storms, a view of the surrounding sea, and fresh water, they were likely to establish a village. They also made temporary subsistence camps where specialized hunting or gathering parties might go at the appropriate season for a particular resource. At the time of European contact, the Unangan population was centered in the eastern part of the Aleutian chain, which has larger

*A deep midden uncovered during excavation of a stratified site on the Alaska Peninsula. Archaeologists have marked the layers they can identify with tags. This profile represents about 8,000 years of precontact time.* (PHOTO BY ELLEN BIELAWSKI)

islands and more coastline available for settlement than do the western islands.

The list of marine resources used by the precontact Unangan is extensive, ranging from large sea mammals—such as sea lions, harbor seals, sea otters, fur seals, and whales—that had to be hunted from boats, possibly with teamwork among hunters, to the intertidal invertebrates—clams, mussels, sea urchins, octopus, and chitons—that even children, the elderly, and the infirm could gather. The people gathered eggs and hunted seabirds such as puffins and murres, as well as ducks and geese. They fished for cod and salmon from the ocean and Dolly Varden and freshwater salmon from streams.

Among the plants available to them, the Unangan very likely used wild rice, wild celery, and crowberries, although these were only condiments to their fish and game diet.

Like subsistence peoples everywhere, the Unangan used all parts of the animal taken in the hunt. Marine mammal bones were sawed, grooved, and incised into harpoon heads, needles, wedges, fishhooks, perhaps spoons, and tools probably used for shoveling. Sea lion hides covered the kayaks that hunters used; these craft were seaworthy enough for the open ocean. People made rain gear from marine mammal intestines, cleaned, split, and sewn together for life in a land that is almost always wet. Precontact Unangan used driftwood in varying shapes for houses, perhaps as wall supports and perhaps inside. They may have hung mats made of beach grass to divide the interior space. Wood probably was cut and carved for other uses but did not survive for very long in the archaeological record. Beach grass was also essential for finely woven baskets and other containers. The people continued to use isotropic stone for flaked knives and points, along with slate and other stone to make oil lamps, projectile points, knives, scrapers, and net sinkers.

Today the Unangan historic and precontact tradition is visible and accessible in at least two

*Archaeologist analyzing stone artifacts on Alaska Peninsula.*
(PHOTO BY ELLEN BIELAWSKI)

places. One is the Alaska Native Heritage Center in Anchorage. The other is Unalaska, where the descendants of this tradition are now centered. There, the Ounalaska Tribe and the City of Unalaska run the Museum of the Aleutians and lead archaeological and oral historical research. Visitors can actually glimpse a bit of the past by visiting or participating in one of the museum's archaeological digs.

Farther east and north of Unalaska, the earliest ancestors of the Alutiiq left extensive archaeological remains on the Kodiak Archipelago and on the Pacific coast of the Alaska Peninsula. As might be expected, all the known sites are well situated for hunting marine mammals and collecting shellfish, or for salmon fishing. These people evolved a material culture similar to the precontact Unangan in bone tools, beginning about 5,900 years ago. Archaeologists assign the remains to the Ocean Bay tradition. Few bone artifacts were preserved, but these sea hunters had by this time developed a barbed-bone harpoon dart head, an artifact that, while it varies in style, is otherwise characteristic of all pre-Alutiiq assemblages. Sea mammal bones recovered indicate that the people hunted sea otters, seals, sea lions, porpoises, and whales. Very little evidence of their dwellings has survived, but it is likely that they used driftwood as wall or roof supports. Even though this evidence is slim, the large numbers of artifacts and debris at Ocean Bay sites suggests that the people lived at least semipermanently at these sites. The best evidence of their lives that we have is in their stone tool kits, which differed in style and workmanship from that of the precontact Unangan. We know from historic and linguistic records that the Alutiiq language was also different from the Unangan.

All the archaeological assemblages from Ocean Bay tradition sites include flaked knives and projectile points, often leaf-shaped. Some of these actually have tapered stems and are triangular rather than oval in cross-section. A variety of scrapers are part of the tool kit, no doubt used to prepare hides for clothing, boat covers, and perhaps for shelter. Stone vessels are rarely found; archaeologists surmise that these were used for burning marine mammal oil for cooking, heat, and light. Some of the Ocean Bay remains include blades that indicate people inherited a blade-making tradition.

By about 3,500 years ago, the material culture of the precontact Alutiiq was changing substantially. The quantity and quality of ground and polished slate tools that people used

*Harpoon dart heads from Kodiak Island (left) and Umnak Island (right) show the similarity of the Kodiak and Aleutian traditions.* (PHOTO BY DON DUMOND)

increased significantly. Such finely honed tools become a hall-mark of the Kodiak tradition, which continues both in the Kodiak Archipelago and in Lower Cook Inlet through the time of historic contact. People sawed, snapped, ground, and polished slate to make knives, adze blades for cutting, projectile points, and ulu-style knives. They made numerous tools, such as harpoon heads, from bone. They also developed toggling harpoon heads, which twist inside the wound hole so the hunter does not lose his prey. They drilled holes through bone, an improvement over the gouging technique of earlier times. Using hard, rough granitic cobbles, people also pecked and ground stone into flat oil lamps. Sea mammal hunters and coastal gatherers, they also relied on the annual salmon runs for subsistence.

As time passed, the Kodiak tradition showed more and more regional diversity in artifact styles among Kodiak, Alaska Peninsula, Lower Cook Inlet, and Prince William Sound groups. The number of sites and their distribution indicates a stable population that grew in size over time. Artistic activity is evident in pecked and polished stone lamps displaying human or anthropomorphic figures, on labrets—facial ornaments worn through pierced skin—and on everyday artifacts such as harpoon heads.

After their emergence from the Ocean Bay tradition, the precontact Unangan tradition and Kodiak tradition evolved in place over the past 1,700 years. After about 700 years ago, the ancestors of the Bering Sea Yup'ik began to expand their range south and southwest over the Alaska Peninsula. They had considerable influence on the Kodiak tradition people, but the precontact Unangan remained essentially self-contained on the Aleutian Islands until Russian explorers arrived in the region after 1741. Russian hunting practices and enslavement and massacres of the Unangan and Alutiiq devastated the people. Nevertheless, descendants of the Alutiiq and Unanagan continue their long, rich cultural tradition today.

# Chapter 3

# Interior of Spruce and Snow: Athabascan Country

*A*way from Alaska's rich coasts with their tumultuous weather, the Alaskan Interior unrolls in range after range of mountains cut by huge rivers. Athabascans traditionally lived along five major rivers: the Yukon, Tanana, Susitna, Kuskokwim, and Copper River. Much of this country is boreal forest, or taiga, seemingly benign compared to the coasts' ice, tides, currents, and storms. Still, above tree line, either to the north or up mountainsides, the Interior is every bit as arctic as the coasts north of the Bering Strait. The fast, cold rivers carry their own hazards: silt from glaciers and mountains swiftly forms and reforms reefs; sweepers—trees that have fallen into the river but remain rooted near shore—wait to snare the unsuspecting boater.

Temperatures in this region are extreme, from 80° to 90°F highs in summer to -40° to -60°F lows in winter. During spring breakup, temperature extremes in one day can raise a river or stream from a trickle to a torrent. Ice dams form, and flood waters rise swiftly behind them. Mosquitoes can drive humans mad in summer, and it was the Interior's debilitating cold that Jack London brought to Outsiders in his story "To Build a Fire."

The Ahtna Athabascans of the Copper River drainage say they were the last Native North American group to be "discovered." Outsiders once called the Athabascan people strangers of the North. Their presence in northern and western North

America presents one of the most intriguing questions in North American prehistory. Before we look at the archaeological evidence (which is scanty at best) that precedes the Athabascan identity in history, we must consider the linguistic evidence of the Athabascan past.

People who speak Athabascan languages reside throughout much of Interior Alaska and on the coasts of Upper and Middle Cook Inlet. The Alaska/Yukon border divides their traditional territory. In Canada, Athabascans reside throughout the Yukon, all of the western Northwest Territories, and in the northern part of the prairie provinces of Alberta, Saskatchewan, and Manitoba. Their traditional hunting territory extends north into Nunavut. Whenever Athabascans arrived in North America, they spread across most of the continent's subarctic forest.

But these northerners are not the only Athabascans. The Navajo and Apache peoples of the American Southwest and smaller tribes (at least historically) living in northern California and Oregon are also Athabascans. How is it that such widely scattered peoples speak closely related languages?

Archaeologists and specialists in historical linguistics have proposed two main hypotheses based on these linguistic connections and in the absence of cohesive archaeological evidence. Basing their estimates on the time it takes languages to differentiate from a common language stock, people speaking an early form of the Athabascan languages might have been present in Alaska's Interior as early as 6000 B.P.

Around 3500 B.P., the Eyak language began to evolve

# Athabascan

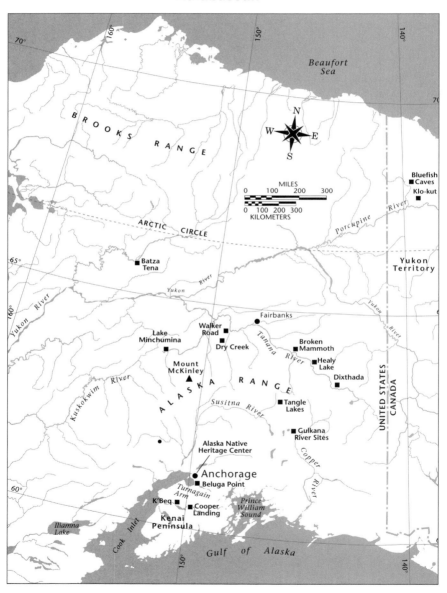

separately from the other Athabascan languages. By the time of historic contact, Eyak was far removed linguistically from all the other Athabascan languages. In structure, Eyak is similar to Tlingit, but Tlingit has an entirely different vocabulary, which may reflect language exchange between the Eyak and Tlingit peoples east and south of the Copper River Delta. By about 2500 B.P., the other Athabascan languages had become distinct. Linguists estimate that people speaking these languages migrated both west, filling Interior Alaska, and south, into British Columbia and presumably as far south as northern California. In a later movement, about 1500 B.P., people speaking what became the Navajo and Apache languages migrated south along the eastern face of the Rocky Mountains. Others went due east, settling in the boreal forest that spreads across Canada to Hudson's Bay and following the Mackenzie River north to tree line, where they likely encountered people who were coast dwellers, precursors of the Inuvialuit who live on the Mackenzie River Delta today. Unfortunately, we have neither oral history nor archaeological evidence that can prove or disprove these suggested sweeping migrations of early Athabascan speakers.

From precontact data, one thing is as clear: Athabascans were culturally, linguistically, and probably genetically distinct from the other four main groupings of Native Alaskans. In fact, one hypothesis about the arrival of people in the New World suggests that the Athabascans arrived, already a distinct group, between the earliest wave of human settlement before 11,500 B.P. (perhaps ancestral to the Tlingit/Haida/Eyak/Tsimshian group) and a much later wave that is directly ancestral to the Yup'ik/Cup'ik, Iñupiaq, and Alutiiq groups. But archaeologists have not been able to connect any early Interior finds in Alaska with any precontact remains in Siberia or northeastern Asia.

In the Tangle Lakes area on the southern slopes of the Alaska Range, east of Denali National Park, four cultural traditions have been recognized so far. These are called the Denali Complex (10,500 B.P.–6500 B.P.), the Northern Archaic tradition (6500 B.P.–1000 B.P.), the Late Prehistoric Period (1000 B.P.–1770), and the Athabascan tradition (1770–present.)

## Tangle Lakes Archaeological District

One of the most accessible and informative areas of Alaska in which to experience precontact life is in the 226,660-acre Tangle Lakes Archaeological District. Here, 400 to 500 precontact sites lie along the southern slopes of the Alaska Range. (Remember: Look, don't touch.) Because this density of known archaeological sites is one of the highest in the United States, Tangle Lakes is on the National Register of Historic Sites. Even a cursory visit makes the attractions of the area obvious. The mountain slopes are ideal for sighting caribou herds and even the solitary moose. Verdant vegetation and a network of tributaries flowing to the Gulkana River mean that migrating caribou pass through during their semiannual migrations. In late summer, the blueberry crop is outstanding in quality and quantity; after the early frosts at this high altitude, the abundant cranberries are a perfect prewinter crop.

The Denali Complex is only slightly later than the earliest Alaska finds at Mesa, Dry Creek, and Broken Mammoth. It is the earliest known occupation of this area. Major environmental changes just preceding the advent of the Northern Archaic would have required either the development of new adaptations or opened the way for people already possessing suitable adaptations to settle in Interior Alaska.

The Northern Archaic tradition dates from about 6,500 to 4,300 years ago at the stratified site of Onion Portage, at what was probably the northwestern-most extension of forest-dwelling peoples' adaptation, but lasts longer in what became the forested Interior. Although the Tuktu site today lies in arctic, rather than subarctic, terrain, it is an early Northern Archaic site. It may indicate that people adapted to the forests of the Interior and moved north along with the forest's expansion. The Tuktu site yielded all of the Northern Archaic attributes along with microblades and tabular microblade cores.

By about 4000 B.P., however, there is a shift in the archaeological record from material culture that can be related to the Northern Archaic tradition to material culture that can be said to foreshadow specific Athabascan cultures that Europeans encountered beginning in the nineteenth century. These likely regional adaptations appear in central Alaska. Sites at Healy Lake, Lake Minchumina, Tangle Lakes, and Dixthada may show the beginnings of a definable Athabascan cultural pattern.

The middle layers at the Broken Mammoth site also belong to the Northern Archaic tradition, as people adapted it to the northern forest. Microblade and burin technology continued from 5000 to 2500 B.P., called the Middle Taiga Period.

Also at Broken Mammoth, the most recent remains fall in a period lasting from about 2500 B.P. to the present. During this time, people stopped using microblade technology at the site. From about 1,500 years ago, the technological tradition leading to Athabascan peoples becomes evident.

Similarly, the Klo-Kut site holds a long, stratified, and dated record of remains leading from the period of regionalization between the Northern Archaic and late precontact periods. People first lived at Klo-Kut about 1,500 years ago. They were primarily caribou hunters who favored hunting in open uplands and in the sparse forest near tree line. Through the layers at Klo-Kut, archaeologists documented the transition from the earliest occupants to a village that is clearly like Athabascan villages were when explorers arrived. Other sites within this time period show that people were harvesting the huge salmon runs on the big Interior rivers, as well as hunting caribou. Common sense again—people in the distant past likely lived much as historic Athabascans did.

Rivers and lakes are the routes through the otherwise impenetrable boreal forest of the Interior. Surely the earliest peoples settled this country by water (just as European explorers did historically). Hauling one's gear is much easier by water. Traditional Athabascans and their dogs walked along shore, pulling sinew lines attached to their loaded canoes in order to travel upstream. Perhaps almost as important, a breeze funneled along a river might provide the only relief from the scourge of mosquitoes during spring and summer.

# Birch-bark Canoes

While Athabascans say their people had different ways of making their essential canoes, all of the craft share a construction that is more complicated than it looks but that yields a beautiful vessel epitomizing the Athabascan adaptation to their land and waters.

Athabascans began the process by making a construction crib in dry sand near water, birch, and spruce trees. They selected and prepared white spruce or birch for the canoe frame, spruce roots for lashing and sewing, birch bark for the cover, and spruce pitch for waterproofing the craft. Some people built their canoes where they could rub the wood against big rocks to shape and smooth it. Other used rough cobbles to sand the wood smooth after splitting it. In precontact times, all of this work was done with stone adzes, axes, and flaked or ground blades.

Inside the crib, the canoe builders—men or women or both—tied canoe ribs of spruce or birch to the temporary posts. Then the builders placed long, split spruce down on the ribs, lashing them with spruce root. To make the bow and stern, they cut white spruce from the base of a tree trunk where it curved into the beginning of roots. People cut birch bark when the sap rose in the spring, rolling the bark inside out and soaking it in water until they were ready to sew it over the canoe frame. Before string, they tied these bark rolls with flexible willow. Gunwales—doubled pieces of split spruce—connected bow, ribs, and stern. When the birch bark wrapped the frame, its edges fit between the inner and outer gunwales; then all three layers were lashed securely together with

### Birch-bark Canoes (cont'd)

more spruce root. Usually women—but often men as well—sewed the strips of birch bark together, using an awl to puncture the bark for each stitch. Finally, the builders applied pitch to all of the sewing holes and seams. Red ochre was used to paint the canoe and may also have acted as a preservative for the craft.

Some canoes were very small, often used by one hunter who poled the vessel in shallow water seeking animals such as muskrat or browsing moose. Some were larger and carried a surprising amount of gear. If the canoe was to carry a heavy load, people covered the bottom with spruce or willow branches to distribute the weight of meat or gear.

Athabascan elder and boatbuilder David Salmon best describes the special place a canoe held in traditional culture: "This is what happens when we finish a canoe: They watch the women sewing the roots. Someone yells, 'Hey, this is the last tie. Everybody come!' It's very important, the last tie they make. People come out of their skin houses and gather around. The last time I made a canoe, there were about thirty or forty people. They circle around and dance, dance, dance. And then we make a speech. We make a speech about the canoe, about the country and how we survived. If it wasn't for the canoe, we wouldn't get food and all that. Without this canoe, we're not going to survive. People from the east, north, west, and south come, and we sing, '*Ha ho*.'"

*Athabascans still rely on the northern forest for many resources when camping on the land.* (PHOTO BY ELLEN BIELAWSKI)

But there is no evidence of watercraft in the first archaeological evidence of habitation in the Interior—variants of the Paleoarctic and, perhaps, Paleoindian traditions. Nor is there evidence of watercraft in the Northern Archaic tradition beginning around 6500 B.P., likely because none has been preserved. While Northern Archaic peoples may be in some ways ancestral to later occupants of the Interior, there really isn't enough evidence to know.

If someone were to design a leave-no-trace lifestyle, they would model it after traditional northern Athabascans. (In contrast, coast dwellers' use of ivory in complex artifacts, and of whale bone in houses and tools, leaves a more substantial, longer-lasting archaeological record than any precontact Interior technology.) A look at their use of spruce, alone, shows how they lived well in what may seem to be a difficult, even hostile environment. People relied on the ubiquitous black spruce for roots that lined baskets and dip nets and for sewing the birch-bark covering onto canoe frames. Spruce gum was used in various states of readiness—soft pitch to cure burns, sores, cuts, and ringworm and to remove cataracts; hard pitch, boiled in water and drunk, as a treatment for cold and flu; chewed into

a salve for sores and held in place with a cambium bandage that was changed every day. Pitch was a hair treatment—it held hair in place, and the wealthy wore it to potlatches— and was used to waterproof baskets and canoes. Spruce

*Stratified layers at the Beluga Point site on Turnagain Arm, just twenty minutes from Anchorage, showed that people of both precontact Athabascan and Alutiiq traditions lived there.* (PHOTOS BY DOUG REGER)

# Footprints of the Past

On the Kenai Peninsula, precontact Athabascans fished the Russian and Kenai Rivers for at least 500 years before contact. Today the Kenaitze tribe invites visitors to two interpretive sites at Cooper Landing, "fishing central" for the salmon sport fishery.

*K'Beq* means "footprints" in the Dena'ina language. K'Beq is the name of both an archaeological site and a boardwalked path along the Kenai River. Kenaitze tribe members guide visitors and explain both traditional local plant use and the archaeological remains. K'Beq also includes a small museum and a shop with Native art, clothing, and books.

At Mile 53.7 of the Sterling Highway, a short self-guided trail begins. It, too, runs beside the Kenai River, leading to a house pit left from earlier Dena'ina use of the area. The trailhead map shows other points of interest along the way.

Other archaeological finds in this area indicate that an earlier people, called the Riverine Kachemak, used this same location and fished the Kenai River from about 3,000 to 1,000 years ago. Archaeologists found more than seven pit houses at a spot on the Kenai ideal for fishing with a drift net. Archaeologists do not know how or why these people "disappeared" in the archaeological record, only that they are replaced by precontact Dena'ina remains. As their name implies, the Riverine Kachemak material culture is similar to that of the Kachemak Bay Culture, the latest phase of the Kodiak tradition in the Alutiiq and Unangan region.

needles burned at the doorway of a tent kept flu away; people inhaled the smoke to treat colds. Eating fresh spruce buds cured diarrhea; pressed onto the skin, the buds eased back strains. Spruce boughs were cut to carpet areas inside tents and in winter around campfires. Tied together, the boughs made good temporary snowshoes.

Similar, extensive use of other trees, plants, and animals of the Interior marked the ingenious, renewable material culture of the Athabascans. This adaptation likely included a deeply spiritual acknowledgment of the land, plants, and animals that made life possible. Although the traces of precontact Athabascans are few and difficult to identify, their adaptation has been lived in one form or another from the beginning of Northern Archaic times, perhaps even earlier.

In terms of their precontact history, Athabascans remain relative strangers to Outsiders. But an understanding of their material culture from historic times to the present shows vividly that Athabascans were in no way strangers in the land they occupied so successfully for at least several thousand years.

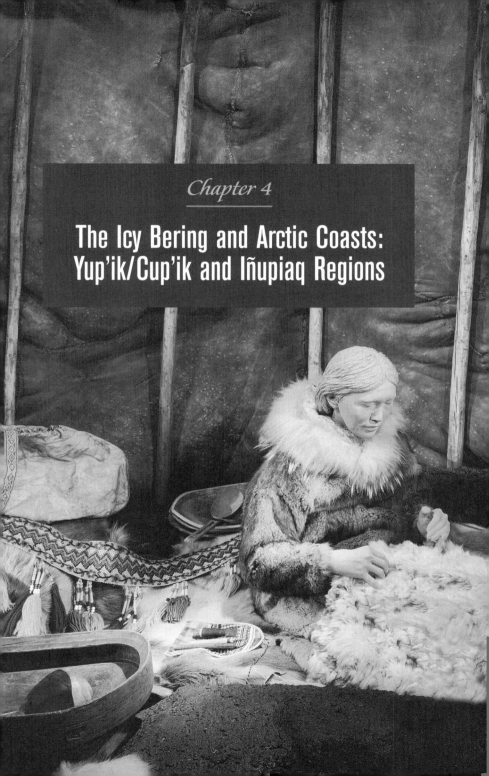

## Chapter 4

# The Icy Bering and Arctic Coasts: Yup'ik/Cup'ik and Iñupiaq Regions

Northof the Alaska Peninsula, through the Bering Strait, north again, and east toward Barrow and beyond into Arctic Canada, the ocean is frozen throughout the winter. The sea ice becomes an extension of the land. Since much of the terrain inland of Alaska's frozen coasts is tundra, the people who lived and still live there needed the means to exploit the resources of a world of windswept, snow-covered, frozen earth or ice.

The people who have called this region home for at least the last thousand years became famous to Outsiders for their astonishing capacity to live well in a place that seems barren to those of us who do not know how to survive there. These people call themselves Yup'ik, Cup'ik, Iñupiaq, and several other variations on these words. Outsiders called them Eskimos. Most popular accounts of the north, in both Alaska and Canada, depict its people living as only some of the precontact Iñupiaq did, only some of the time: dwelling in igloos and eating raw meat. The full range of Yup'ik, Cup'ik, Iñupiaq, and related adaptations are far more complicated than this simplified picture. This range of adaptations has its ancestry in ancient cultures alive at least 2,000 years ago and may trace some elements to even earlier cultures.

Because all of the Yup'ik, Cup'ik, Iñupiaq, and related peoples shared many elements of common ancestry, as well as an environment of tundra and frozen coasts, the archaeology of

# Iñupiaq
# St. Lawrence Island Yupik

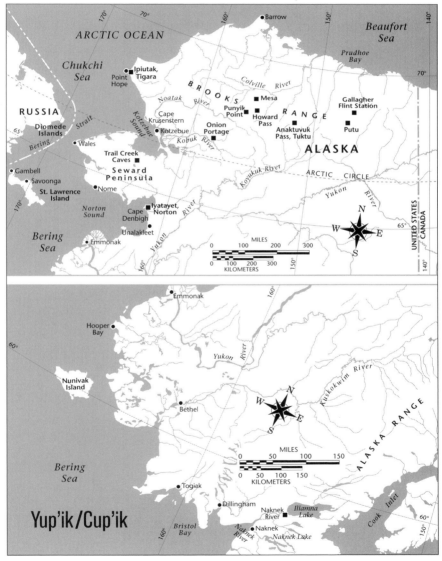

two present Native regions is covered together here in one chapter. In one way, however, the Yup'ik/Cup'ik region, which extends from the north side of the Alaska Peninsula to the south side of Norton Sound and inland approximately 300 miles, differs substantially from the Iñupiaq region farther north. The southern boundary of Yup'ik/Cup'ik territory borders the Alutiiq/Unangan region along the Alaska Peninsula. It is evident that throughout prehistory, people on both the Pacific Ocean and Bering Sea sides of the peninsula interacted with each other across the peninsula. Their actions created a very complex archaeological record. As yet, there is not enough evidence to know for sure who was influencing whom at any given time before contact.

Prior to 5,500 years ago, the archaeological record of the Yup'ik/Cup'ik and Iñupiaq regions parallels that elsewhere during Beringian times. Other than at Trail Creek caves on the Seward Peninsula, there are no remains that date earlier than about 12,000 B.P. (Recall that some researchers believe that the Trail Creek broken bone could have resulted from natural processes rather than human manufacture.) Before about 5500 B.P., remains from this area share in the Paleoarctic tradition, apparently carried throughout all of what was once tundra Alaska.

Regional specification in the archaeological record begins on the frozen coasts around 4,500 years ago, with the appearance of the Arctic Small Tool tradition (referred to by archaeologists in shorthand as ASTt). The ASTt does not appear to be a direct lineal descendant of the Paleoarctic tradition;

rather, the Paleoarctic tradition was interrupted and replaced by the Northern Archaic tradition throughout much of Alaska. The ASTt is the first *archaeological culture* that appears to be the remains of people who developed a tundra-maritime adaptation in Northeast Asia, migrated to the northwestern coasts of Alaska, and continued to spread east across coastal Arctic Canada. As such, the ASTt represents the first adaptation to what later became, historically, Yup'ik, Cup'ik, and Iñupiaq territory. People bearing this material culture were caribou hunters. Although there is as yet no evidence that they used boats or the technology to hunt seals through their breathing holes in the sea ice, the ASTt people may well have had a good grasp on marine mammal hunting. The archaeological record also yields no evidence that they harnessed dogs for hauling sleighs, as the later historical Yup'ik, Cup'ik, and Iñupiaq did. Yet, between about 4,500 years ago and 3,000 years ago, people using a distinctive tool kit of small microblades, cores, burins and burin spalls, thumbnail-size scrapers, and bifacial projectile points spread out of northeast Asia all the way to Greenland.

In Alaska, the first ASTt artifact assemblage came from Cape Denbigh, on Norton Sound almost due east of Nome. The tool kit, first named the Denbigh Flint Complex, displayed outstanding stone workmanship on the smallest of flakes, which were sharpened to make small curved knives, or flaked on both sides and pointed at both ends. These blades were likely the end or side blades inset in bone or antler projectile points or knives. Later excavations at the Punyik Point site in the Brooks Range, and comparison with similar assemblages all across the central and eastern Arctic, led archaeologists to group the Denbigh Flint Complex within the broader Arctic Small Tool tradition.

Most of the Alaskan ASTt sites consist of the remains of temporary campsites, either on the coast or along inland watercourses but still on the tundra. Very few sites contain the remains of more permanent house structures, probably built for use during the winter. All of these are inland, at sites such as Onion Portage on the Kobuk River, Howard Pass in the Brooks Range, and on the upper courses of the Ugashik and Naknek

*The excavated remains of an Arctic Small Tool tradition house pit on the Alaska Peninsula. The house probably had four corner roof supports. The dark central area was a fire pit. Discarded fire-cracked pebbles, probably heated in the fire and then dropped into cooking containers that held soup or stew, form a pile next to the hearth.* (PHOTO BY DON DUMOND)

*Stone tools of the Arctic Small Tool tradition and the Norton tradition, all from the Alaska Peninsula. The distinctive small size of the ASTt projectile points, upper left, shows clearly in comparison to the Norton projectiles, upper right. Below, two large Norton projectile points and one side blade.* (PHOTO BY DON DUMOND)

Rivers, both on the Alaska Peninsula. Thus far, the greatest number of dwellings has been found and test-excavated on the upper Naknek River drainage.

The Naknek River dwelling remains are roughly square, measuring about twelve feet on each side, with what was probably a tunnel entrance on one side. Inside some dwellings, vertical stone slabs might form a central cooking area; others have only piles of fire-cracked rock near the remains of a fire. The houses were dug into the ground up to one and a half feet

# Beach Ridge Archaeology: Cape Krusenstern National Monument

**A**rchaeological research usually requires excavating. That's why sites are called "digs." Generally, material on or near the surface of a site is the youngest; the deeper you dig, the older the material you find. But on Cape Krusenstern history isn't vertical, but horizontal. There, on the Chukchi Sea about forty-five miles north of Kotzebue, 114 beaches have formed through wave, current, and wind action on the shore over about 9,000 years. Precontact peoples camped on the beaches nearest the sea in their time. Now, the oldest archaeological remains are on the oldest

*The aerial photograph shows Cape Krusenstern with many of the beach ridges clearly visible. The map is the result of many archaeological surveys and excavations at the cape. It took years to map archaeological remains and to understand the passage of time and people there.*

(COURTESY OF THE NATIONAL PARK SERVICE)

beach, well inland of the current shore, while Native people still hunt marine mammals off the present-day shoreline. Between the oldest and the youngest beaches lie remains from the Denbigh Flint Culture and the Choris, Norton, Ipiutak, and Western Thule Cultures. Surveys and excavations at Cape Krusenstern, led by the remarkable scientist J. L. Giddings over many years, contributed to mapping the chronology of precontact occupations on the Bering and Chukchi Seas. Above Cape Krusenstern, remains from some of the earlier peoples of Alaska lie on even older terraces.

Cape Krusenstern National Monument is also a Native hunting ground and the summer nesting place for thousands of migratory birds, drawn by the lagoon and pools between some of the beaches. The area is accessible by boat or aircraft from Kotzebue.

and probably were covered with sod chunks as well as animal hides. At Onion Portage, the ASTt semisubterranean houses are round, usually with a large central hearth lined with stones. A house structure at Howard Pass is similar in shape to those on the Naknek River.

Arctic Small Tool tradition people lived and hunted in the Interior primarily for caribou and perhaps somewhat less so on the coast for seals. Alaska Peninsula sites have been located primarily along rivers, and some faunal evidence indicates people were there to take advantage of the large salmon runs.

The disappearance of the ASTt people from the archaeological record is still a puzzle. They apparently withdrew first from the northern part of their territory, north of the Brooks Range, and eventually, around 3500 B.P., even on the Alaska Peninsula, where their population density was probably greater than in regions farther north. Archaeologists do not know why or how the ASTt people left the region or if their material culture simply changed over time. One school interprets the data as indicating a slow, sporadic evolution of some aspects of the ASTt into the later precontact cultures of the region. Another school interprets the data as indicating that the ASTt people disappeared entirely, relatively suddenly, leaving a clear hiatus in the archaeological record.

In the latter interpretation, the absence of ASTt people left open the way for a "general cultural reorientation" (in the words of scholar Don Dumond in *The Eskimos and Aleuts*) that led eventually to the Yup'ik, Cup'ik, and Iñupiaq cultures that existed when European explorers arrived in their land. Many archaeological sites and assemblages that demonstrate this cultural development are grouped in the Norton tradition. This grouping of sites and artifacts includes several others known from excavations that took place early in this region: Choris Culture, classic Norton Culture, and Ipiutak Culture. Norton tradition people showed decreased use of microblades and fashioned projectile points that are larger and more leaf-shaped than those of the ASTt people, as well as burins of different forms than those of the earlier people. A major change came with the use of pottery for the first time. This crude ware was tempered with fiber such as grass and stamped with linear designs before being fired at a temperature just high enough to solidify the clay. The pottery is very similar to pottery found in northeast Asia at the same time and earlier. Gradually, the pottery style changed from a linear design to a check-stamped pattern that archaeologists regard as definitive of the Norton Culture around 2500 B.P.

By about 2500 B.P., the Norton people seemed to have focused their lives on settlements along the coast, shifting their general emphasis from inland caribou hunting to greater reliance on maritime hunting. In places, this allowed the estab-

*A carved ivory pottery paddle from the Norton tradition at Point Hope is in the collection of the University of Alaska Museum, recently renamed the Museum of the North. The design is different on each side of the paddle so that the pot maker could vary the pattern while shaping the soft clay of a pot. The check-stamped pattern is more common in Norton ceramics than the linear design.* (PHOTO BY DON DUMOND)

lishment of permanent coastal communities that were occupied repeatedly and frequently, if not continuously.

In the remaining precontact millennium in this region, the archaeological record is enriched due to the remarkable preservation of bone and ivory artifacts in frozen soil. No other matrix in Alaska preserves artifacts so well. Archaeological sites are also much more visible on the coast and tundra than in the forests of the Interior and Southeast. On the basis of this rich record, archaeologists have been able to define more specific archaeological cultures than we see anywhere else in Alaska. We do not have enough evidence from other regions or earlier times to know if the cultural specificity and artistic fluorescence evident north of the Bering Strait during the last 1,500 years is paralleled elsewhere in Alaska.

On the Bering Sea Coast, the Norton tradition lasted until about 1,200 years ago, when the Thule Culture superseded it. While the Thule Culture grew on the Bering Sea and farther north, Norton tradition influence still extended across the Alaska Peninsula to the Pacific Ocean side. There, Norton traits are still evident in the Kodiak tradition of the Alutiiq region around 1,400 years ago. Farther north, the most recent stage of the Norton tradition is seen in the Ipiutak Culture. Ipiutak, near the current village of Point Hope, is the type-site for the Ipiutak Culture, which lasted from about 2000 B.P. until about 1,200 years ago.

The Ipiutak site held the remains of hundreds of permanent houses and unusually lavish burials. Unfortunately, the artifact assemblage and grave goods at the site attracted extensive site

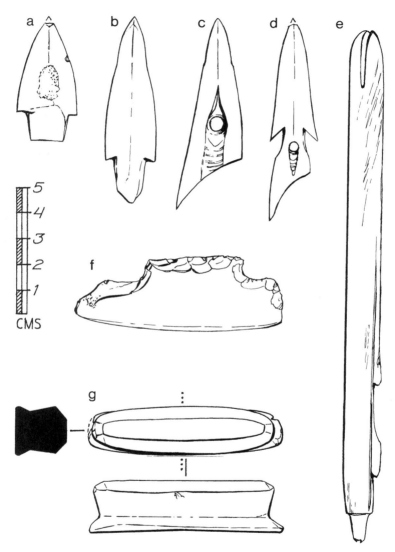

*Thule tradition artifacts: a and b, polished slate projectile points;*
*c and d, ivory toggling harpoon heads; e, a projectile head made of antler*
*with a slot to hold a polished stone end blade; f, an ulu made of polished slate;*
*g, a mouth-size labret, made of coal, to be worn through a pierced opening in the skin.*

(ILLUSTRATION BY CAROL STEICHEN DUMOND)

looting early on. Ipiutak shows the influence of Asian cultures of the same time, especially in its art.

The most recent archaeological tradition on the frozen coasts, the Thule Culture, began about 1,000 years ago. It is directly ancestral to the Iñupiaq, Yup'ik, and Cup'ik peoples and is the basis for the lifeway that Outsiders think of as "Eskimo," whether in Arctic Alaska, Arctic Canada, or Greenland.

On the Siberian side of the Chukchi Sea and on St. Lawrence Island, a sequence of archaeological cultures developed beginning about 2,000 years ago that is remarkable for its artistry as well as its emphasis on open-water hunting. Archaeologists named the earliest of these archaeological cultures Okvik–Old Bering Sea. The assemblages consist of polished slate, pottery tempered with fiber, and dramatically decorated harpoon heads of bone and ivory. Like those of the Kodiak tradition far to the south, these are toggling harpoon heads. The Okvik–Old Bering Sea Culture may have evolved out of the Norton tradition, but evidence of this transition is still lacking in the archaeological record.

Over the past millennia, Okvik–Old Bering Sea evolved into a culture called Punuk on both the Asian and Alaskan shores of the Bering Strait. At the same time, Ipiutak Culture held sway on the north coast of Alaska until changing into a significantly different but descendant culture called Birnirk. Also during that period the Norton tradition remained evident on the Alaska Peninsula. All of these variants lead in some way to the Thule tradition, which is widespread by about 500 years ago.

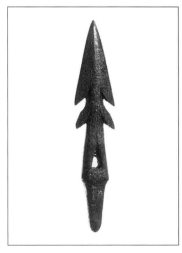

*Late Thule tradition artifacts. The dart head (upper left) and the sealing harpoon head (plan view and side view) are made of antler. The large whaling harpoon head is made of whale bone with a slate end blade. The carving of a small head on a rod is made of ivory.* (PHOTO BY DON DUMOND)

## Umiaqs—Open Skin Boats

The immediate ancestors of the Iñupiaq, Yup'ik, and Cup'ik developed an adaptation to their ice-bound coasts that separates them from earlier people who lived in the area. Along with small kayaks, the most recent precontact coastal people built and used large skin boats called *umiaqs* that could carry several people and their property.

*Kayak builder Noah Andrew with seal skins stretched for drying near Kwigillingok.* (PHOTO BY CLARK JAMES MISHLER)

The Thule people, like the early ASTt people 2,000 years earlier, must have had roots originally in Asia. Having gradually settled along both the Russian and Alaskan shores of the Bering Strait, a group or groups—archaeologists usually use the specific label Thule Culture for them—migrated along the coasts of Arctic Alaska, Arctic Canada, and Greenland. The Thule adaptation was based on hunting in open water or among floating ice pans from kayaks and umiaqs (see sidebar)

Umiaqs (called *angyapik* by the St. Lawrence Islanders) were used to move from communities to summer camps, for visiting between camps, and for whale hunting. In fact, the umiaq and the whale hunt are probably inseparable in the culture and history of northwest Alaska, St. Lawrence Island, and the Bering Sea region.

Precontact and historic umiaqs were made of a driftwood frame covered with walrus hide. Bearded seal hide was made into lashing line. Walrus and seal were hunted in late winter so that the hides could be stretched and dried in the spring light and wind. The thick walrus hides were split into two layers so that each hide provided double the coverage of an unsplit hide. Men and women worked on splitting the hides. Men built the umiaq's frame using a curved piece of driftwood for the bow, then setting the keel and stern. Then they steamed driftwood to make the boat's curved ribs. Finally, women sewed the walrus hide over the frame.

Umiaqs may be paddled, but sails made of walrus gut or seal skin were used traditionally. Yup'ik elders estimate that a walrus-skin boat under sail can travel at speeds up to fifteen knots.

and hunting seals at their breathing holes on solid ice during winter. The Thule people used dogs both to carry gear and in traction to pull sleighs. The people settled coastal sites, where large, partly underground structures with roofs supported by whale bone and driftwood indicate a level of permanence and comfort not indicated for earlier, more nomadic peoples of the frozen coasts. During the first 500 or so years of their existence, the Thule people seem to have emphasized

# Bering Strait to Greenland

## *Migration, Language, and the Foundation for Life on the Arctic Coast*

By the beginning of the twentieth century, explorers, whalers, traders, and missionaries had been telling their peers—for nearly 300 years—about the people who lived on the Arctic Coast of North America. But no one knew, back then, that all the people from the Bering Strait region, throughout Canada's Arctic Archipelago, along the shores of Hudson Bay and Labrador, and around the coast of Greenland were essentially one culture, one

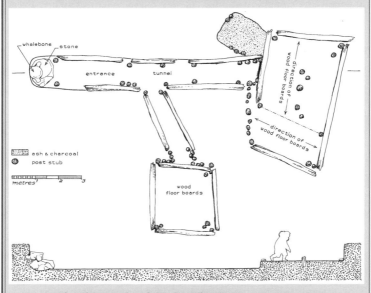

*Drawing of the remains of a Thule tradition house on Cape Krusenstern. Whale bone and driftwood were both used in the structure. Charcoal lay all over the floor of the smaller room, leading archaeologists to believe it was a "kitchen."* (ILLUSTRATION BY CAROL STEICHEN DUMOND)

group of people who all spoke mutually intelligible dialects of the same language. Knud Rasmussen, a Greenlander who was part Greenlandic Inuit and spoke their language, made this discovery when he spent two years traveling west from Thule, in northwest Greenland, to Barrow, Alaska, in 1923–24. This was the last in a series of research trips that Rasmussen, six other researchers, and Inuit assistants made to determine what was then called "Eskimo origins." It was called the Fifth Thule Expedition, so named because Rasmussen and coleader Therkel Mathiassen established their base among the Polar "Eskimo" at Thule, Greenland. The Fifth Thule Expedition provided the scientific basis for all subsequent research into Thule Culture archaeology, as well as superb documentation of the Iñupiaq and Inuit way of life early in the twentieth century.

communal hunting of large whales, as many Alaskan Iñupiaq still do today.

While they are known as whale hunters, Thule people and their descendants continued to rely on caribou and other terrestrial resources and on the salmon runs of Alaska's great rivers. From their coastal base, they expanded into some interior areas of the North Slope, the Brooks Range, and along rivers such as the Kobuk and Noatak. Through trading relationships and travel, the Thule Culture even influenced the Pacific cultures of the Alutiiq on Kodiak Island and around the Gulf of Alaska.

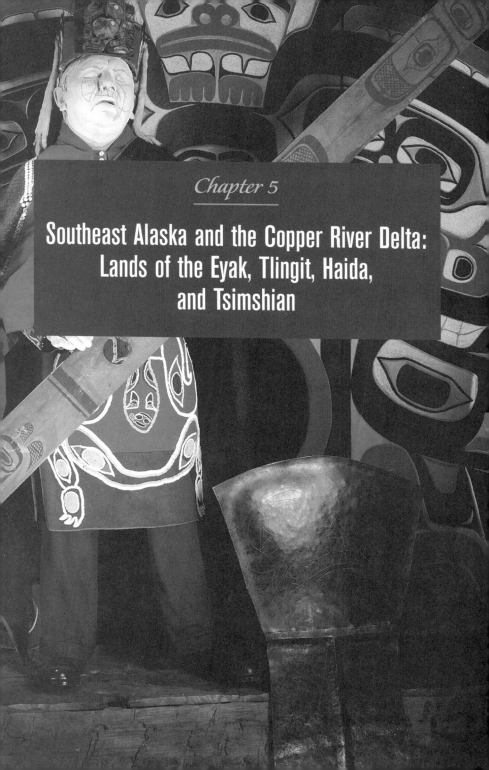

# Chapter 5

# Southeast Alaska and the Copper River Delta: Lands of the Eyak, Tlingit, Haida, and Tsimshian

*S*outheast Alaska is a narrow but dramatic temperate rain forest located on both islands and shore, between the wide-open Pacific and the summit of the Coast Mountains. To the east lies the dry, cold interior of Canada's British Columbia and Yukon. To the north, the sheltered waters between the outer islands and the Inside Passage open into the unsheltered Gulf of Alaska and the exposed shores beneath the enormous Yakutat Glacier and many other ice tongues. The Southeast region, so different from the Arctic of the Yup'ik/Cup'ik and Iñupiaq, and the subarctic lands of the Athabascans, is home to the Eyak, Tlingit, Haida, and Tsimshian peoples.

The Eyak, whose nearly extinct language has the structure of an historic Athabascan tongue, but a vocabulary like the Tlingit language, live at the mouth of the mighty Copper River. It is the main waterway through Athabascan country southeast of the Alaska Range, south of the Wrangell Mountains, and east of the Chugach into the Gulf of Alaska. Yet the closest Eyak ties are with the Tlingit.

In Beringian times, the Southeast coast was heavily glaciated. Yet, there were refuges, oases of land and water where people with watercraft, knowledge, and the right tools could live. Some archaeologists hypothesize that this coast was the main trail to settling the New World, as long as 30,000 years ago. No evidence here stretches back to that early date, but finds far south in Chile may. If people arrived in southern South America that long ago, we must keep open the possibility that they boated along Alaska's Southeast coast.

# Eyak, Tlingit, Haida, and Tsimshian

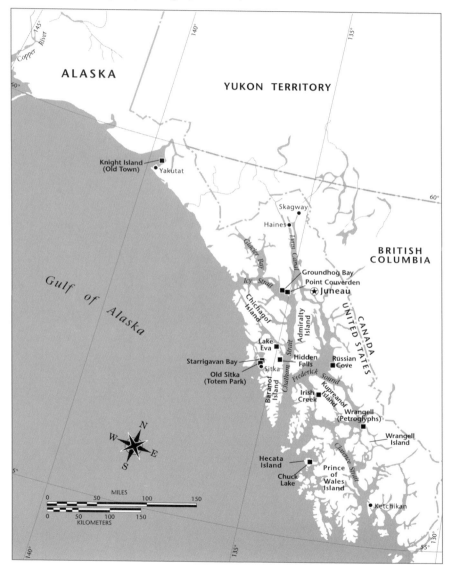

# Petroglyph Beach State Historic Park

*Petroglyphs on the beach near Wrangell.*
(PHOTO BY ANDROMEDA ROMANO-LAX)

One of the most intriguing Southeast archaeological sites is within walking distance of downtown Wrangell. Boulders among the beach gravel bear designs and figures that were pecked into these boulders with stone tools.

The age and origin of the petroglyphs are unknown. People have studied the spirals and faces, trying to connect them with the present-day Tlingit residents or their immediate ancestors. Some people believe the petroglyphs were made by a group of people with a culture completely different from that of the precontact Tlingit. There is no method to determine their age and thus connect them with dated sites in the area's precontact history. We do know that the petroglyphs are slowly wearing away, from both weather and everyday exposure to people who used the beach before the site was protected by law. Since the petroglyphs were first counted, almost two-thirds of them have disappeared, leaving only about forty that are especially clear when the boulders are wet. Two "new" petroglyphs came to light during construction of the interpretive walkway, however, to the delight of locals. Replicas of several petroglyphs are on the boardwalk to the beach so people can take rubbings of the designs rather than increase wear on the originals.

The archaeological evidence along this coast begins, however, only 9,500 years ago, with a tool kit that resembles the Paleoarctic artifacts from elsewhere in Alaska. Archaeologists call this regional variant the Paleomarine tradition. It is a core and blade stone industry that includes microblades and burins. Bone and antler projectile points, with slots on each side to hold side blades, are also found. "Wet" (waterlogged) sites may preserve artifacts for several thousand years longer than the acidic soils of boreal forest sites, and archaeologists have been fortunate to excavate at least one very deep, stratified site. It lies near what is now Prince Rupert, British Columbia. In Alaska, the Paleomarine tradition is dated to approximately 9500 B.P. at sites such as Groundhog Bay, Hidden Falls (the early component, called Component II), and Chuck Lake.

Between 6500 B.P. and 5000 B.P., artifact assemblages show a transition from late Paleomarine tradition types into a developing Northwest Coast tradition. During the transition phase, microblades and unifacial flaked stone tools decrease in number, while ground stone tools appear and increase in number. Lake Eva, Point Couverdon, and Irish Lake are known transitional sites.

By 4,670 years ago, Component II at Hidden Falls had a well-developed ground stone industry. Sites that belong to this phase also lie on Hecata Island, Prince of Wales Island, and Traders Island. At this time, a signature feature of the Southeast Alaska archaeological record appears: large, deep middens that are primarily the discarded shell remains of clams, chitons, and other shellfish that clearly had become an important part of

## A Well-preserved Find

**N**ative people throughout Alaska relied on baskets as traditional containers, variously weaving them from spruce root, beach grass, strips of willow, or birch bark. Archaeologists are sure that such "soft" material culture was essential to precontact peoples.

A few years ago, people boating along the southern tip of Baranof Island came upon the remains of a basket that was rapidly eroding out of a river-bank. Alert to the significance of the find, and especially to its fragility, they notified museum professionals and archaeologists, who quickly dispatched a conservator and an archaeologist to the site. The professionals were able to stabilize the basket and remove it, along with a good deal of its wet earth context, to the conservation lab.

*Fragments of ancient basketry at the Alaska State Museum in Juneau.*
(PHOTOS BY STEVE HENRIKSON)

This basket was eventually dated to 4490 B.P. It is made of hemlock root and branches, and its design is markedly different from the traditional basketry style and technique known from

*Model of an ancient basket based on a reconstruction drawn by Delores Churchill, a Haida weaver, from the basketry fragments.*

Southeast Alaska. Another rare and fortuitous find, a spruce root basket from Prince of Wales Island, has been dated to 5300 B.P. While neither basket is complete, the conserved fragments hold many clues about precontact basketry. When conservation is complete, the fragments will become part of the permanent collection at the Alaska State Museum in Juneau.

precontact peoples' diets. This preserved shell evidence, which shows that people were skilled at harvesting intertidal resources, leads archaeologists to the conclusion that people also collected and used a wide variety of sea plants, such as bull kelp, sea urchins, blennies, and sea cucumbers. Crabs and snails, whose soft shells don't preserve in the archaeological record, were also likely part of the precontact diet. Of course, fish—salmon, herring, halibut, lingcod, and rockfish—birds, both seabirds and inshore dwellers, and marine mammals—sea lions, harbor seals, sea otters, and porpoises—were also available.

In short, from about 5,000 years ago, people along this coast were exploiting food resources so abundant that they established large winter villages as a focus for all this gathering and fishing. Such large settlements were likely also supported by specialized subsistence camps where people went to fish, hunt, or gather a specific food and then bring it back to a village.

As time passed, people probably intensified their use of prime coastal sites. Component III at Hidden Falls is dated to 3,000 to 1,300 years ago and shows continued use of bone and stone technology. The number of known sites increases during this time, which may reflect growth in a stable population. However, most of the known sites that archaeologists have found from this period are seasonal subsistence camps.

In the late phase of the developing Northwest Coast tradition, the remains of large structures appear in the archaeological record. Archaeologists interpret the sites with such houses as permanent winter villages. The structures were probably the precursors of the cedar houses that Tlingit and Haida people used in historic times. Other sites in the late phase show remains of hunting, fishing, and gathering of sea mammals, deer, fish, shellfish, and berries. Some of the tool kit maintains the artifacts well-known from earlier phases—ground stone and bone projectile points and knives, along with flaked obsidian. People were making and using new items as well: stone bowls and lamps and native copper made into blades of all sorts. New styles are evident in the harpoon heads. Sites dated to this phase have been found at Groundhog Bay, Starrigavan Bay (just north of Sitka), Russian Cove (on the mainland), and Knight Island.

Archaeological evidence in the northern part of the region shows similarities with historic Eyak culture. This, along with linguistic evidence, indicates that Eyak territory extended farther south and east in late precontact times than it did at the time of contact with Europeans. Linguistic evidence also indicates that the Eyak and Haida peoples had a close relationship from about 2,000 years ago up to a time of Tlingit expansion—as recently as within the last 300 years—from inland out onto the coast. Tlingit oral history and some archaeological evidence indicate that ancestors of the Tlingit have been on their land for

10,000 years, or "time immemorial" as oral history puts it. The Haida have been resident, in their view, on the Queen Charlotte Islands (in Canada) also from time immemorial. A group of Haida moved north to the Prince of Wales Island area in what is now Alaska during late precontact times. Tlingit moving from inland to dominance on the coast between Icy Bay and Prince of Wales Island may have ruptured a close link between Eyak and Haida peoples.

In 1741, the Russian explorer Vitus Bering reached the northwest coast of Alaska. Over the next half century, Eyak and Tlingit people encountered Russians in pursuit of sea otter pelts, as well as British, French, and Spanish explorers. The Russians established their fort at Sitka (just south of the pre-contact occupation at Starrigavan Bay, which is now the site of the Alaska Marine Highway ferry terminal) in 1799. The Tlingit, resisting Russian control, destroyed the fort in 1802. All of this history is accessible in and around Sitka, from precontact sites and some of the few remaining old-growth cedars, to the Russian fort in the present town, and south to Totem Park, which is centered on the Tlingit/Russian battlefield.

Most of the Tsimshian people live between the Nass and Skeena Rivers in British Columbia, Canada. In historic times, the Tsimshian dominated the rich trade between interior and coastal British Columbia and Alaska. Late migrants to what is now Alaska, a small group of Tsimshian moved into the southeasternmost islands of Alaska in 1887 in part because of the population disruptions caused by the epidemic disease and conflict of the historic period.

## Cedar Canoes

Only in the temperate rain forest of the Southeast region did trees grow large enough to serve as the sole raw material for watercraft. The large cedar of the area provided much to the people, and the people, in turn, honored and cared for the cedar. The first step in carving a dugout canoe was a ceremony to ask the "tree people" for

*Master Carver Wayne Price and helpers steaming a cedar canoe to widen its center and raise the bow and stern.* (PHOTO BY CLARK JAMES MISHLER)

The Eyak, Tlingit, Haida, and Tsimshian peoples all share in what is called the Northwest Coast tradition. Supported by the abundant and stable resources of the sea, intertidal areas, and coastal rain forest, Native peoples of the Pacific Northwest coast from the Copper River Delta all the way south to Oregon developed a complex social system. It included the potlatch, a gathering of people and distribution of gifts held to mark life events and changes in leadership; a complicated system of family one of their members to be taken and made into a canoe.

Once the tree was chosen, cut, and stripped of bark and branches, carvers hollowed out the inside of the trunk. Then they added pieces to the bow and stern, thwarts, and gunwale rails. The larger canoes had masts for sails made of woven grass or bark mats.

The last step in making the craft ready for the sea was steaming. This required volcanic rocks—abundant in Southeast Alaska—that were heated red-hot in a fire topped with the cedar wood that had been removed while carving the canoe. Burning this "heartwood" was believed to give life back to the new boat from the old tree.

The canoe was wrapped (in canvas or, in earlier times, bark or hide) and filled with salt water. Then the hot lava rocks were placed inside the canoe, and the wrapping was closed, holding the steam inside. When the canoe cooled, the wrapping was opened, the cool rocks were removed and returned to the fire, and fresh hot rocks were placed inside the canoe. This process was repeated until the bow and stern rose as the canoe widened and its bottom flattened. Canoe steaming was (and still is) a great occasion, involving hard work, cooperation, and spiritual preparation and guidance.

organization, including clans and rigid marriage rules; widespread trade both up and down the coast and over the mountains into the Interior; and warfare and slavery. The archaeological sequence in Southeast Alaska shows the material features of this culture in the remains of large villages, comprised of longhouses that could shelter between twenty and fifty people, and sites that could be defended against enemy attacks.

Historically, the Tlingit dominated the main trade route to

the Interior through what is today called Chilkoot Pass. The Tlingit in fact used that famous "gold rush" trail for centuries, if not millennia, before the Klondike gold rush that brought the Tlingit homeland to the attention of the rest of the world. Since that time, the Eyak, Tlingit, Haida, and Tsimshian peoples' spectacular art and design, sophisticated clan and leadership systems, and remarkable adaptation to the ocean and rain forest have become renowned.

# Recommended Reading and Resources

The text for this book draws on the following publications, which range from technical summaries for professional archaeologists to guides for everyone. It is also easy to become better acquainted with ancient Alaska through your library and online resources. Alaskan museums and information-center Web sites can direct you to publications about specific regions and to opportunities to participate in or visit archaeological digs. In person or online (see Web sites below), start with the Alaska Native Heritage Center in Anchorage, where Native Alaskans can introduce you to their traditional cultures and provide information about local activities around the state.

## Books

Damas, David, ed. *Arctic.* Vol. 5 of *Handbook of North American Indians.* Washington, D.C.: Smithsonian Institution Press, 1984.

> *A comprehensive, scholarly summary of the origins, adaptations, and history of the arctic peoples.*

Dumond, Don E. *The Eskimos and Aleuts.* London: Thames and Hudson, 1987.

> *Meant for professionals and therefore thorough, but highly readable with excellent illustrations. Essential to integrate Yup'ik/Cup'ik and Iñupiaq past and present lives.*

Gabriel, Moses. *Gwich'in History: The Handed Down, Oral History of Alaska's Gwich'in People of the Fort Yukon Area.* Fairbanks: Yukon/Alaska Publishing Company, 1993.

> *Very readable oral history from the farthest north Athabascan country.*

Garza, Dolly A. *Surviving on the Foods and Water from Alaska's Southern Shores.* Marine Advisory Bulletin 38. Fairbanks: University of Alaska, 1989.

> *Fun to use and a good way to grasp how well precontact people of Southeast Alaska knew and used food sources in their environment.*

Giddings, James L. *Ancient Men of the Arctic.* New York: Alfred A. Knopf, 1973.

> *Despite its age, this is still the best book for anyone interested in Alaskan archaeology and how archaeologists researched our present understanding of Alaskan precontact history. Very well written, as Giddings weaves the story of his discoveries with the stories of past and present peoples.*

Halliday, Jan. *Native Peoples of Alaska: A Traveler's Guide to Land, Art and Culture.* Seattle: Sasquatch Books, 1998.

> *Although several years old, this book remains a useful guide for visitors who are specifically interested in Native sites and activities. The appendices on continuing Native subsistence living and on the Alaska*

*Native Claims Settlement Act and Native Corporations also put many common questions into a sound historical framework.*

Helm, June, ed. *Subarctic.* Vol. 6 of *Handbook of North American Indians.* Washington, D.C.: Smithsonian Institution Press, 1981.

*A comprehensive, thorough, and scholarly summary of the origins, adaptations, and history of the subarctic peoples.*

Kari, Priscilla Russell. *Tanaina Plantlore, Dena'ina K'et'una.* Fairbanks: University of Alaska, Alaska Native Language Center, 1995.

*Scholarly and thus reliable, a wonderful book to carry with you when exploring Athabascan country, much of which is within driving distance of Anchorage and Fairbanks. Clear descriptions, drawings, and photographs.*

Kawagley, Oscar. *A Yupiaq Worldview: A Pathway to Ecology and Spirit.* Prospect Heights, Ill.: Waveland Press, 1994.

*A clear and concise description and analysis of Yup'ik thought and practice.*

Langdon, Steve J. *The Native People of Alaska.* Anchorage: Greatland Graphics, 1993.

*A brief, useful summary of Native cultures from the time of contact forward.*

Layton, Robert, ed. *Conflict in the Archaeology of Living Traditions.* London: Unwin Hyman, 1989.

*Academic, but useful for anyone interested in the intersection of*

indigenous interpretations of the past and archaeological interpretation of material culture.

Luke, Howard (ed. by Jan Steinbright Jackson). *My Own Trail.*
Fairbanks: Alaska Native Knowledge Network, 1998.
Oral history of traditional and contemporary Athabascan life from the
twentieth century and earlier.

Napoleon, Harold (ed. by Eric Madsen). *Yuuyaraq: The Way of
the Human Being.* Fairbanks: Alaska Native Knowledge
Network, 1996.
An original, thoughtful analysis of how epidemic diseases between
1770 and the mid-twentieth century changed traditional Alaska Native
cultures forever.

National Museum of Man. *The Athapaskans: Strangers of the
North.* Ottawa, Ont.: National Museums of Canada, 1974.
The catalogue to a remarkable exhibit of Athabascan crafts, clothing,
and tools.

Pratt, Verna E. *Alaska's Wild Berries and Berry-like Fruit.*
Anchorage: Alaskakrafts, 1995.
A small, easy-to-use guide to the many berries Alaska Natives knew
and used.

Ritter, Harry. *Alaska's History: The People, Land, and Events of
the North Country.* Portland, Ore.: Alaska Northwest
Books, 1993.
A concise and readable history of Alaska that begins with contact
between Alaska Natives and newcomers.

Smith, Kathleen Lopp, and Verbeck Smith, eds. *Ice Window: Letters from a Bering Strait Village 1892-1902.* Fairbanks: University of Alaska Press, 2001.

> *A remarkable collection of letters written from Northwest Alaska, rich in description of daily Iñupiaq life of the time.*

Steinbright, Jan. *Qayaqs and Canoes: Native Ways of Knowing.* Anchorage: Alaska Native Heritage Center, 2001.

> *A visual treat and storyteller's joy, this book documents traditional boatbuilding by craftspeople from each of the five Native Alaska regions who gathered at the Alaska Native Heritage Center in 2000 to replicate their ancient designs.*

Viereck, Eleanor G. *Alaska's Wilderness Medicines: Healthful Plants of the Far North.* Portland, Ore.: Alaska Northwest Books, 1998.

> *Good technical descriptions and clear drawings of Alaskan plants used for traditional Native medicines.*

## Periodicals

Morgan, Lael, ed. "Alaska's Native People." *Alaska Geographic* 6 (3) (1979).

"Prehistoric Alaska." *Alaska Geographic* 21 (4) (1994).

"Dawn of Humans." *National Geographic* 198 (6) (2000):40-67.

## Public Information Brochures

The following brochures are available at many visitor centers and museums, including the Public Lands Information Center in downtown Anchorage, where many books and maps are also available.

*Fossil Collecting and Artifact Hunting in Alaska: What is Legal, What is Not.* State of Alaska (Office of History and Archaeology) and Bureau of Land Management (Alaska State Office), n.d.

*Save Alaska's Heritage, A Disappearing Treasure: Archaeological Resource Protection, Artifacts, Fossil Ivory and Bone.* National Park Service, Archaeological Assistance Program, n.d.

*Save Alaska's Past: The Archaeological Resources Protection Act.* National Park Service, n.d.

## Web Sites

The Web site of the Alaska Native Heritage Center in Anchorage provides detailed history and cultural description for the five major regional Native groups of Alaska, as well as a guide to the center, its programs, and links to other useful sites: www.alaskanative.net.

The National Park Service maintains several linked Web sites that include archaeology and history as shown in the national parks. Alaska has many parks, and the NPS provides summaries of Alaska prehistory online:

www.nps.gov/akso/akarc

www.cr.nps.gov/archeology.htm

www.americashistoricplaces.com/historyalaska/index.htm

The following Web sites list the current programs of Alaska's major museums and provide links to other useful sites and places:

www.museums.state.ak.us

www.museumsalaska.org

www.aleutians.org

www.anchoragemuseum.org

www.uaf.edu/museum/

# Index